T0329519

THE ENDURING ADVISORY FIRM

The Bloomberg Financial Series provides both core reference knowledge and actionable information for financial professionals. The books are written by experts familiar with the work flows, challenges, and demands of investment professionals who trade the markets, manage money, and analyze investments in their capacity of growing and protecting wealth, hedging risk, and generating revenue.

Since 1996, Bloomberg Press has published books for financial professionals on investing, economics, and policy affecting investors. Titles are written by leading practitioners and authorities, and have been translated into more than 20 languages.

For a list of available titles, please visit our Web site at www.wiley.com/go/bloombergpress.

THE ENDURING ADVISORY FIRM

How to Serve Your Clients More Effectively
and Operate More Efficiently

Mark Tibergien
Kim Dellarocca

To Arlene Tibergien, Mark's wife, companion, and rock for over 35 years.
To Nico Dellarocca, the best thing that has ever happened to his mother, Kim.

Contents

CHAPTER 9
Investing Women

PART III: BRINGING CHANGE TO YOUR PRACTICE

CHAPTER 10
Transforming from Practice to Business

CHAPTER 11
Culture Wars

CHAPTER 12
A Vision and Leader for the Future

Index

Acknowledgments

We consider ourselves fortunate to have found work that is fulfilling and challenging. Through our combined 60-plus-year journey we have learned a lot about the kinds of investments firms need to drive success. Above all we have learned that the most important investment one can make is in others. We have learned that the quality of our relationships is the biggest driver of our happiness and success. We have learned to slow down, to be present, to think win-win, and to do our best to build others up. We have learned that sharing our talents and wisdom matters, often most to those individuals whom we may never meet. We have learned to let go and laugh more. We have learned that friendship promotes the happiness of all.

We are grateful to include here a small list of those friends who have lent their wisdom and inspiration to the book, provided coaching and opportunities along our path, and been the people we most enjoy simply sharing a laugh over a bottle of wine. They are:

The members of the Pershing Executive Committee, especially Lisa Dolly, Jim Crowley, and Caroline O'Connell.

The members of the Pershing Advisor Solutions Executive Committee, in particular Karen Novak, Gabe Garcia, Ben Harrison, and Evan LaHuta, and the incredible team of professionals who make this company a great place to pursue our career objectives.

Our clients and friends, Gerry Tamburro, Jim Pratt-Heaney, Andy Reder, Ross Levin, and the Pershing Advisor Council, for opening their businesses to us to study and for sharing their experiences.

The provocative thinkers who inspire us: John Hagel, Cam Marston, and Philip Palaveev.

Our families, friends, teams, and colleagues who supported us in achieving this as well as so many other important goals.

John Wiley & Sons and our editor, Christina Verigan, for their help, focus, and flexibility.

We would also like to thank each other. We have had an enduring friendship for many years, and our efforts to put this book together did not compromise our relationship as some had predicted—rather they made it stronger.

Mark Tibergien and Kim Dellarocca

Preface

Financial services firms have long operated independently. The 1980s ushered in two variations on existing business models that accelerated the growth of the entrepreneurial mindset in which practitioners became owner/operators instead of working as employees of another firm: Registered Investment Advisors (RIA) and Independent Contractor Broker/Dealer (IBD) reps.

Now we are seeing a couple of new dynamics: first, the transformation from practice to business; second, the emergence of multi-owner/multi-employee advisory firms. In this light, the notion of independence becomes a bit murkier because there are more mouths to feed, more constituencies to please, and more competition for strategic direction from multiple points of view. While ownership may be independent, the notion of making decisions without the influence of others is less true.

That said, RIAs are the purest form of independence in that they are free of broker/dealer oversight and overrides on their compensation, whereas the IBD model is subject to supervision by the broker/dealers with whom they affiliate and they must share an override on their revenue production with the broker/dealers. There is also a difference in approach to business as recognized by their different regulatory structures, i.e., the SEC vs. FINRA: the RIA model is composed of professional buyers whereas the IBD model is composed mostly of professional sellers, meaning that in the former, they get paid directly by the clients and act as fiduciaries or client advocates on all accounts; whereas broker/dealer reps get paid on a grid for the products they sell and for the most part operate under a suitability standard, though a recent ruling by the Department of Labor will change that condition for retirement accounts.

There has been some morphing of these identities in the past decade, however, as many IBD reps have either formed their own RIAs or became Investment Advisor Representatives (IAR) of their broker/dealer's corporate RIA. (Those who are registered reps and have their own RIA are known as Hybrid Advisors while those who operate under the supervision of their broker/dealer's corporate RIA are known as Dually Registered).

This background is important for understanding the transformation of the retail financial advice business and the catalyst for growth. Not only is there a big shift from brokerage to advisory, from transactional to fee revenue, or suitability to fiduciary, but from single books of businesses managed by solo practitioners to larger, professionally managed practices, many operating in multiple locations.

Perhaps the biggest leap in the evolution of independent advisory businesses is the shift from small to medium-sized firms. Consider this: The U.S. Small Business Administration (SBA) regards Financial Investment firms (NAIS Code 523) such as securities brokerage, portfolio management, investment advice, or trust & fiduciary firms as small businesses when their annual revenue is below $38.5 million. An advisory firm with $1 billion of assets charging an average of 80 bps would be generating under $10 million of annual revenue, so to exceed the small business threshold, an advisory firm would need to be managing somewhere between $3 and $4 billion of assets. While there are few who fit into that mid-sized category of advisory firm today, it is clear it won't be long before there is a meaningful cluster of such firms with more and more merging, acquiring, or growing organically to a new level of critical mass.

Just a decade ago, for example, it was a big deal for independent advisory firms to achieve $1 billion of assets under management (AUM). According to Evolution Revolution, produced by the Investment Advisor's Association in March 2015, more than half of all SEC-registered advisors have AUM between $100 million and $1 billion. Today, there are more than 3,000 RIA firms that manage more than $1 billion of assets (Figure P.1). Even more significant is that according to the 2016 Investment News Study on Compensation & Staffing sponsored by Pershing Advisor Solutions, there are now more employees within advisory firms than there are owners. Few things mark the emergence of a real business than this dynamic.

FIGURE P.1 Number of SEC-registered investment advisors above and below $1 billion real assets under management in 2015

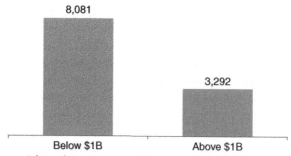

Source: Investment Advisors' Association, Evolution Revolution 2015

For many firms that have become bigger, it may feel like those of us over 35 who seem to add a pound for every year we are on the planet. It's insidious, it's persistent, and it's maddening. Principals in larger advisory firms look around at their holiday parties and wonder how the guest list got so big! It is a management dilemma to experience challenges inherent in being a small practice but with the added complexity of a larger business.

Growth of these firms has come organically for the most part with the addition of new staff and new advisors. In other cases, growth came through mergers or acquisitions. Oftentimes, the growth was not conscious but merely reactive to the increasing demands for their services as their brands became stronger and their value became more appreciated.

Over the years, we've come to recognize that advisory firms hit a series a walls when they add more staff, almost in accordance with the Fibonacci sequence (a pattern of numbers where each number is the sum of the two preceding numbers). They hit a wall at 5 people, 8, 13, 21, and so forth. By hitting a wall, I mean that quality control, staff supervision and management, and the client experience each get strained.

In this scenario, each advisor seems to have their own approach to working with clients, developing recommendations and in some cases, even in how they produce reports. But far worse than applying a different approach to clients is when teams of individuals form cliques to pursue and serve clients a specific way for a specific need that is different from the firm's stated strategy. Often there is no consistent method of training, of quality control, or of staff development. The unevenness ultimately hurts the firm brand because clients are having distinctly different experiences depending on with whom they work. Even certain employees feel disadvantaged if they are on a team that is less productive or effective than another.

The good news is that the strain is caused by business growth and therefore the problem is eminently fixable. The bad news is that partners and employees often grow attached to their way of doing business so changing their behavior requires mutual sacrifice for the good of the enterprise.

When advisory firms evolve from small to medium size, relationships get strained and profitability suffers. But like adolescence when your clothes don't fit and mood swings become more frequent, one must conquer the awkwardness that this brings. When you hit the wall, ask the right questions: Is my strategy still relevant? Am I structured right to achieve my strategic goals? Do I have the right people doing the right things? Am I clear on what success looks like? Are we all in agreement about the goal and how we get there?

With this book, we have attempted to take a fresh look at the business of financial advice. Clearly, much has happened since the pioneers in financial services climbed the mountains and swam the streams to find a new and effective way to help individuals achieve their financial goals. The early leaders in this movement had less of a desire to work with partners and employees than the people coming into this business today. But that leaves the next generation of leaders at a loss as to what successful business models look like.

In our opinion, there are five key characteristics that the best-performing advisory firms share:

1. Clear Positioning—they know who their optimal client is and create a client experience in alignment with this insight.
2. Structural Alignment—they design work flow, leverage technology, and build processes that allow them to serve their clients effectively while running their businesses efficiently.
3. People Planning—they strive to match the right people to the right jobs and create an environment where motivated people can flourish.
4. Actively Manage to Profitability—instead of viewing financial performance of their business as a consequence of their actions, they use the levers of financial management consciously to produce the right outcome.
5. Systematic Client Feedback—they incorporate a process that allows them to elicit from their clients insight into what's on their minds—not just whether they are satisfied but whether they are fulfilled and at peace with the direction they are heading.

As you read this book, we hope you will be able to recognize the different ways we suggest for incorporating these five elements into your thinking so that you can build a business to last.

Mark Tibergien and Kim Dellarocca

PART I

The State of the Advisory Business

CHAPTER 1

Key Business Trends

Assumptions

Back in the day when individual investors were buying stocks and bonds instead of packaged solutions like mutual funds and ETFs, there was an investment analyst Mark knew in Seattle who was locally famous for his contrarian bets. His inclination was to look at companies currently out of favor with the investing public; assess their management, their culture, and their market; then take a long view of their business to determine whether it was an opportunity worth owning.

The stockbrokers who worked for this particular firm adored the man, whom we will call "Conan the Contrarian," because his reverse approach always made them look good with their clients. Today, whenever we hear some industry pundit spout conventional wisdom, we try to channel Conan. We find it helpful to ask, "What would Conan do?" whenever we see our profession fleeing from or toward an idea.

Among the beliefs most often repeated are:

- Advisors are reducing their fees.
- Young employees lack a work ethic.
- Robos/digital platforms will make it difficult for advisors to compete.
- The industry will benefit from a huge generational transfer of wealth.

There are many more, of course, but we examine these questions in light of the facts and the reality on the ground. No doubt, our opinions will stir the

3

ire of some but that's exactly what Conan would do—cause people to challenge convention, then act with the wisdom they've gained from the analysis.

Advisors Are Reducing Their Fees

While there are a number of advisors who claim to be experiencing some fee compression, we have found that the top-performing advisory firms have actually increased their fees in each bracket of client. Much has been written about fee compression in the industry but we struggle to find signs of such a trend. In fact, in 2010, the yield on AUM (revenue divided by AUM) was 78 basis points, compared to 77 in a 2014 study and 75 in the 2015 study.[1]

It appears those firms most under pressure are the ones whose value proposition is tied to investment performance. There are also some wealth management firms who have had more difficult conversations in the past year with clients who are experiencing percentage returns of less than 5 percent.

Those who have raised their fees claim they have had very little attrition because they have been able to demonstrate value beyond the investing relationship and even beyond the basics of financial planning. They may be giving their clients unique access to private banking or alternative investments, or they are creating a community of clients in which others want to be part.

As we have learned from observing other industries that have been commoditized (for example, coffee, retail grocery, medicine, tax accounting), those who can command a premium are those who can deliver a premium experience and who are perceived to be offering more value.

Young Employees Lack a Work Ethic

It is a curious claim among industry elders that it is a challenge to find young people who work as hard as they do. Having interacted with thousands of advisors over our careers, we would agree that advisors born in the Baby Boom era tend to value motion over movement and equate time in the office with hard work. But the amount one perspires is not a measure of perseverance.

Gen X, Y, and now Z employees seem to eschew the illusion of industriousness created by their forerunners as they seek more balance in their life to pursue other interests and devote time to their important relationships. They consistently ask their bosses to evaluate them on output, not input. This is a

---

[1] *Investment News*, "The 2015 Investment News Compensation and Staffing Study," October 18, 2015. Available at: www.investmentnews.com/section/specialreport/20151018/COMPSTAFF.

very difficult mindset for founders of advisory firms whose blood, sweat, and tears created their practices and resulted in the advisory business as we know it today.

Over the past couple of years, we have observed a number of advisory firms transferring to the next generation with little fanfare and minimal disruption. Firms that seem to be growing the fastest according to surveys done by *Investment News*[2] and *FA Insight*[3] have been investing in better hiring, retention, and development programs to ensure business continuity and stronger growth.

Fortunately, many business leaders in this industry will acknowledge that the old way of managing through carrot and stick may not be as effective as creating opportunities for personal growth, recognizing that the desire for employees to have a life outside work, investing in their career development, and rewarding fairly does pay off. The challenge is that such a systematic approach requires more disciplined management, which frankly, is not the job that most advisors aspired to when they formed their own practices.

Robos Will Make It Difficult to Compete

Every decade presents new obstacles and new challenges for financial services. Mark started in this business in the 1970s just before the disappearance of fixed rate commissions. Since then, we've also seen a number of other disruptors.

Off the top of our heads, we think of the RIA custody model, the self-directed platforms, the emergence of ETFs and index mutual funds, rebalancing software, and account aggregation as examples of ideas that caused disruption to different segments of the business. At Pershing alone, which is the largest securities clearing firm in the United States and a division of the largest custodian in the world (BNY Mellon), we have seen advisory assets grow from 5 percent of our total in 2007 to more than 50 percent today.

Furthermore, we have seen regulatory reform influence how many conduct business in the United States as well as overseas. In the United Kingdom, for example, with the introduction of the retail distribution review (RDR), platforms may no longer obtain reimbursements from the fund companies for whom they provide access to advisors and their clients. This has forced a new economic relationship between all the parties, but has also created greater transparency in costs and deliverables. In Australia, the Future of Financial

---

[2] Ibid.
[3] FA Insight Study of Advisory Firms: People and Pay and Growth by Design Studies.

Advice (FOFA)[4] requires advisors to tell their clients what they can expect to pay in actual dollars for the services to be rendered in the coming year. Now that these financial professionals cannot hide the charges clients are charged, they have to do more to demonstrate value.

The point is that robo-advisors—or digital platforms—are just another step that automates what was a manual and labor-intensive experience. Using algorithms, their model portfolios may even be able to outperform the strategies that human advisors deploy. But this is not the only reason why individual clients choose to work with a financial professional.

The complexity of a person's life—especially the wealthier they are—requires judgment and insight. What clients want is an easier way to access these points of view along with a simpler way to conduct business. For most advisors, leveraging technology to deliver the best of robo combined with the best of humans will likely be the model for advisory firms. Of course, the pure technology plays will get their share of business just as the self-directed platforms at places like Schwab, TD Ameritrade, and Fidelity have. The challenge and the opportunity for advisors is not to concede that ground to those investing so much in competitive solutions, but rather partner with providers who can enhance the client experience while at the same time keeping the advisor at the core of the relationship.

The Profession Will Benefit from the Pending Transfer of Wealth

Depending on what you read, you will find there is upward of $40 trillion of wealth in the United States alone that is expected to go from the Baby Boomer generation to their children and grandchildren.[5] As a result, pundits are urging advisory firms to create a process for capturing this asset movement by positioning their firms properly in the minds of the inheritors and their benefactors.

While money in motion can be great for those prepared to be in the middle of it, the reality is that most of this wealth will be distributed in fractions to their beneficiaries. And not all of the beneficiaries will be the offspring of the rich folk. Much of this will go to charities and other causes the creators of wealth hold dear. Bill Gates (Microsoft) and Mark Zuckerberg (Facebook)

---

[4] http://asic.gov.au/regulatory-resources/financial-services/future-of-financial-advice-reforms/fofa-background-and-implementation/.

[5] Accenture Consulting, "The 'Greater' Wealth Transfer: Capitalizing on the Intergenerational Shift in Wealth," 2015. Available at: https://www.accenture.com/us-en/insight-capitalizing-intergenerational-shift-wealth-capital-markets-summary.

are great leading examples of people who want to make an impact with their legacy. Their kids will also see a large inheritance upon the death of their parents, of course, but the point is that what is left over will be distributed in much smaller chunks.

Furthermore, the suggestion that advisors should be on a death watch waiting for their Baby Boomer clients to croak is insulting to younger prospective clients. The greatest amount of wealth creation will come from the efforts of Gen X, Y, and Z directly. We are seeing great examples of innovation and consequently wealth accumulation that has little to do with being born with a silver spoon.

So the opportunity for growth from inheritance is a very dark strategy when one considers the opportunity for growth from betting on the next generation of wealth accumulators. A balanced approach seems to be the best strategy.

While skepticism about conventional wisdom is healthy, your wariness will prove useless if you don't take a constructive approach to what you perceive as threats. Being a professional naysayer adds little value to business decisions.

Granted, there are many other examples of conventional wisdom that deserve challenge. They at least deserve to be questioned as we observe a profession that is going through one of its most profound changes in decades. Advisory firms of the future, however, will not be replicating each other's business strategies, but will be challenging convention, deciding based on facts, and finding cracks in the market that will result in big openings to do more business.

What Should You Consider?

That's why it is so critical to review what you know about the business and try to understand what the data and trends are telling you about its future, and your role in it.

There are several irrefutable facts that should be informing the strategies for leaders in financial services.

- The business is experiencing margin compression.
- Growth for mature firms is coming more from existing clients than new.
- There is an oversupply of clients and an undersupply of people to provide advice.
- The industry in general has a tarnished reputation among prospective employees and clients.

- Compliance and regulation is a growing component in a firm's financial statements.
- Industry consolidation is inevitable as age and economics drive owners of advisory firms to make difficult choices.

Margin Compression

At a time when the average advisory firm is growing and the average advisor is making more money than ever, it is not always obvious when an advisory firm is suffering profitability challenges. This is why we recommend that advisory firms maintain proper financial statements with key ratio reports that show trends in gross profit margin and operating profit margin.[6]

Profitability in advisory firms is affected by several forces. Earlier in this chapter we rebutted the notion of price compression for the best-performing firms, but the reality is that the average advisory firm has not been able to keep the prices aligned with their rising costs of doing business or adjusted for the added services an advisory firm may be delivering to clients. Furthermore, with most fee structures tied to asset values, it is difficult for many advisory firms to keep pace with inflation in a low-return environment.

In addition to pricing, five other variables that affect profitability the most are:

1. Poor service mix
2. Poor productivity
3. Poor client mix
4. Poor cost control
5. Low revenue (sales) volume

In our experience, most advisory firm leaders do not actively manage to profitability and as a result are unaware of the insidious nature of some of their decisions. For example, it is common to introduce new services or take on new clients because of a perceived opportunity, not because of a conscious strategy. As a result, substantial resources and attention get diverted to a new initiative that costs more than it generates.

The advisory firm of the future will need to be more disciplined about the investment decisions it makes in its own business, much like it creates a framework for making investment recommendations for clients based on risk, reward, diversification, and other drivers.

---

[6] Mark C. Tibergien, *Practice Made (More) Perfect: Transforming a Financial Advisory Practice into a Business* (Hoboken, NJ: Bloomberg Press, 2011).

Growth for Mature Firms

As advisory firms evolve through their life cycles, they take on the same characteristics as the humans who manage them. In the early years, it runs on energy, not on wisdom. In the teen years, the firm acts with an insouciance derived from the belief that nothing bad can happen. When it arrives at adulthood, the business acts with confidence and wisdom. In the later years, its energy begins to wane and the decisions that emanate from the business seem to be focused on conserving rather than growing.

For advisory firms that have not invested in the development of people, it reaches a limit in regard to the number of active client relationships that can be served effectively. Depending on what is being delivered and how the clients are being served, that limit is somewhere between 50 and 150 clients per advisor.

Once advisors reach capacity, they tend to slow their efforts to develop new business. In firms containing multiple professionals, all with responsibility for getting new clients, this is not a concern. However, in firms in which all the advisors have reached their peak, it's not uncommon to see revenue from new clients drop from 15 to 20 percent of the total to 5 to 10 percent.

Why is this a concern? Often in parallel with the aging of the advisor is the aging of the client. There comes a point that with limited renewal of the client base, most clients shift into withdrawal phase away from accumulation. The old rule of thumb was that investors could afford to withdraw 4 percent of their wealth in order to live their lives comfortably. Assuming this as your guide, and assuming your revenue is tied to assets under management, advisors would need to replace these assets each year just to stay even. But of course, this gives no consideration to death or termination of the client relationships, let alone the rising costs of doing business.

It is clearly important for advisors to define reasonable growth objectives in clients, assets, and revenues, and manage them all to a goal. Without a conscious target, it is possible to become complacent about the need to refresh one's center of influence, seek out referrals, and urge everyone in the firm to be aware of the need to grow each year.

An Oversupply of Clients, an Undersupply of Providers

Every industry would love the unique dynamics of the financial profession. Throughout the world, we have seen a marked increase in the number of millionaires. Simultaneous with this trend, we are seeing a decline in the number of advisors guiding these individuals whose lives have become more financially complex.

For example, in the United Kingdom since the implementation of Retail Distribution Review (RDR) in 2013, 10,000 independent financial advisors (IFA) have left the business. In the United States, since the market collapse of 2008, there are 40,000 fewer financial professionals in all channels.

Many of these clients are seeking do-it-yourself (DIY) solutions that they can obtain online, but there is still considerable demand for the wisdom and insight that come from working with a professionally trained advisor—especially when their decisions go beyond the investment realm.

The talent shortage is a risk for advisory firms that are seeking to grow because it is more difficult to find the right people to do the work they seek. It also means that compensation costs are rising in order to create the right inducements for people to join these organizations.

The talent shortage is also an opportunity for advisory firms that are able to position themselves as the employer of choice in their markets. They can establish a presence on college campuses where personal financial planning or related disciplines is a legitimate major. They can recruit from other firms by promising a career path, an opportunity to work with more challenging clients, and the appeal of greater financial rewards.

For advisors contemplating the future of their business in a sea of uncertainty, being positioned clearly among prospective employees and partners creates an opportunity unique in our business.

Tarnished Reputation

In a recent survey, most investors believe the financial services industry puts profits ahead of client interests.[7]

The reputation of financial services has diminished a lot over the decades. The financial crisis of 2008, the nefarious activities of players like Bernie Madoff and his compatriots, the mortgage crisis, the collapse of previously trusted financial institutions have all contributed to a negative image. Even those who have held themselves out as fiduciary advisors got caught in the mix, with several leading advisors being indicted and convicted for illegal behavior.

As much as Main Street advisors try to distance themselves from the stink of corruption, both the trade press and Main Street media highlight the misdeeds of people in the business constantly. Furthermore, members of Congress and regulators persistently cite the abuse of elders and the less informed as reasons to tighten the rules on bad behavior.

---

[7] http://blog.aaii.com/most-investors-believe-financial-services-industry-puts-profits-over-client-interests/.

Of course, it doesn't help that industry regulators have diluted the terminology, thus making it difficult for the average consumer to truly understand whom they are dealing with. For example, the term *advisor* was meant to be the province of those registered with the SEC but when broker/dealers purloined that nomenclature as a replacement for the term broker, no one objected. Yet broker/dealers operate under an exemption that says their registered reps can give advice as long as it is incidental to their business. Imagine holding yourself out as an advisor without having to register as one because it's not considered core to what you do.

Other terms that tend to confuse is fee-only versus fee-based. Or suitability versus fiduciary standard. If you are the average client without reason to understand the jargon of this business, it may come as a surprise to you when you are recommended or sold something that doesn't fit your goals, your risk profile, or your level of comprehension.

This is not to imply that one segment of the business is less trustworthy than another. It would be as if a chiropractor held himself out as an osteopathic doctor. Chiropractors and osteopaths are both medical professionals who treat patients with a focus on the musculoskeletal system. But the two disciplines require different levels of certification.

A chiropractor is a medical professional trained in chiropractic medicine, typically in a three to four year program. An osteopath, on the other hand, must be a licensed physician and is able to perform surgery and prescribe medicine.

The parallel to financial services is that clients do not know if they are being served by someone who gets paid based on the products they sell them, or paid for the advice they give regardless of which financial solution they use. Furthermore, when a bad act is committed, the press usually uses the word "advisor" in the headline, which reinforces the idea that the entire business is suspect.

In the end, advisors and brokers who are able to convey confidence and trust and who are transparent in how they conduct business will go a long way toward giving comfort to clients, prospects, and centers of influence. But the apprehension people have in dealing with financial services providers remains a headwind in the conduct of business.

Compliance Costs Are Rising

Regardless of which business model financial professionals operate under, the cost of compliance continues to rise. For independent firms, this cost can represent 2 to 4 percent of all expenses. For the most part, it is a variable cost, meaning that it goes up and down based on the volume of business one is doing.

Much of what has to be done in the advisory profession is prophylactic and not to remedy bad deeds, but the cost of surveillance and enforcing rules of behavior is meaningful. To be effective, it requires at least one individual whose sole job is to monitor activities and take remedial actions when something is amiss. It's like having a traffic cop on every corner.

Most advisors would say they are honest and ethical, so the cost of compliance seems especially burdensome. But the myriad rules in place to ensure both brokers and advisors are acting in the best interests of their clients require well-trained specialists to educate, inform, and direct partners and employees to stop, look, and listen before acting.

Consolidation Is Inevitable

All of these forces of change contribute to the need for advisory firms to become bigger. "Bigger" is a relative term, of course, since for the most part, advisory firms are small businesses, even micro businesses.

But complexity and costs require firms to be managed professionally. Adding layers of process and management to a business means that revenues also have to increase to cover those costs. The need to generate more requires the addition of people and thus begins a never-ending cycle of growth.

Many firms have grown naturally by adding layers as needed, but others have found benefit in merging[8] with like-minded firms to more efficiently consolidate certain costs, gain operating leverage, and establish a bigger market presence more quickly.

Firms like Hightower moved quickly to create a semi-national Registered Investment Advisory firm focused on recruiting people out of wirehouse brokerage firms. Focus Financial was an early roll-up firm that has acquired numerous large advisory practices around the country though it has not tried to merge them into a singular brand or common client experience. Middle-wear providers such as Dynasty serve as a bridge between advisors and their providers, providing outsourced solutions to those not yet big enough or disciplined enough to create their own management infrastructure for this purpose. Numerous advisory firms throughout the United States and in other countries have merged, as the founders of one looks to retire but seeks to provide continuity to their employees and clients.

---

[8] www.fa-mag.com/news/mergers-and-acquisitions-continue-on-pace-21238.html.

While we do not predict the end of the solo-practitioner, it is clear that there will be a divergence in size and presence in different markets. It is not unfathomable to see some truly national advisory firms much like we see in the accounting profession with its Big 4 CPA firms. More likely, we will see the emergence of super regional advisory firms—what the accounting profession labels as "Group B" firms.

These super regional advisory firms will be managed professionally with a branch manager system not unlike the brokerage industry. While there will be some that are scattered across the frontier, more likely the best-performing super regional firms will have a geographic concentration that provides for tighter management, tighter branding, and operational leverage.

We expect there will also be smaller, local advisory firms that find value in banding together with other advisors to create some economies of scale and continuity of practice. Many of these will be formed by second- and third-generation advisors who do not have the same fear of working with others that many of the industry pioneers seemed to have.

What the Assumptions Mean for You

One thing is clear in any business: What got you here will not get you there. In our mind, this means that the assumptions about the advisory business over the past 100 years have changed dramatically.

Think of what has transpired since the 1970s alone.

In 1975, fixed commissions, which were the standard of practice for brokerage firms for decades, were eliminated. Discount brokers such as Schwab, Scottrade, and TD Ameritrade (Waterhouse) emerged as major players in the delivery of financial products. Many well-known brokerage firms subsequently went out of business.

This was one of the catalysts for the creation of the independent broker/dealer movement, in which registered reps were switched from being employees to becoming independent contractors. Their average payout went from 35 percent to 82 percent, which changed the economics of many broker/dealers.

Late in that decade and into the 1980s, the retail-oriented Registered Investment Advisor (RIA) emerged along with new support models, which we have come to know as "custodians." These custodians, like Schwab, TD Ameritrade, Fidelity, and Pershing Advisor Solutions, replaced institutional brokers and providers by wrapping in technology, practice management support, and service teams as well as best execution capabilities. Today, the RIA segment represents almost $4 trillion[9] in total assets, or roughly 20 percent of the U.S. retail market.

In the 1990s, no-load mutual fund platforms emerged, in which advisors could get access to packaged products for no commission payments. This reduced the cost of access. So, too, did the emergence of index funds provided by the likes of Vanguard and Dimensional Fund Advisors.

In the early part of this century, ETFs emerged as a threat to the mutual fund model because of its liquidity and low-cost appeal. Once again, traditional providers were undermined and the custodians saw their margins compressed as the revenue went from 12(b)1 fees provided by the mutual fund companies to their fund supermarkets to transactional revenue.

The point of this short history is that change has proven to be the one constant in financial services.

It is clear that client attitudes, technology, staffing requirements, business economics, and regulation are once again challenging leaders in this business to conceive of business models that will be competitive, profitable, and sustainable for the long term.

How the landscape has changed will inform the strategies of every firm, but not every firm will deploy the same strategy. At least they shouldn't. The ideas presented throughout this book will help you clarify and deploy your strategy. We will stress the importance of tried and true business management principles—have a vision, know and serve your client well (the ones today and tomorrow), and inspire leadership at every level.

We have tried to narrow broad best practices and view their implications on the business of financial advice. We seek to provide actionable ideas to prepare the leaders of financial advisory businesses and advisors for the future, ensuring that they are clear on their optimal client, new ways to differentiate from their competitors, and their definition of success.

---

[9] The Cerulli Report: "Advisor Metrics 2015. Anticipating the Advisor Landscape in 2020."

CHAPTER 2

What Business Are You In?

A former colleague of ours who moved on to a new role developing strategy at one of the UK's leading wealth management firms introduced us to Simon Sinek's book *Start with Why*.[1] His book proved to be a powerful catalyst to begin asking every advisor we meet about their *why*.

The query itself may remind us of the insistent and annoying strings of questions we hear from young kids, but forcing an answer gives clarity to our decisions. Too often in business, we hear people tell us what they do and how they do it. There is a heavy emphasis on the mechanics of what we do. But rarely do the answers touch us emotionally. Ultimately, we need to understand why we should care.

Imagine that your prospects, clients, employees, and vendors are asking the same questions about you. How would you respond?

This is your mission should you choose to accept it:

- Why do prospects come to your firm and why should clients stay?
- Why do employees join your firm and why should they stay?
- Why do you believe your business exists?

These questions prove very hard to answer for many. We have a tendency to respond with features and benefits. We emphasize what we do rather than

---

[1] Simon Sinek, *Start with Why: How Great Leaders Inspire Everyone to Take Action* (New York: Penguin, 2009).

who we are. We don't talk about the communities we are connected to, but the solutions we provide. When you think about it, anytime we hear others prattle on about their business in a way that sounds remarkably familiar, our eyes glaze over. Almost every advisor's website says something like, "We provide comprehensive wealth management tailored to your needs." That is truly yawn-worthy, isn't it?

What Sinek believes is that great companies don't lead with the "what and the how," but an unyielding belief in their purpose, their mission, and their cause. He says, "People don't buy what you do, but why you do it."

When I read Sinek's book, it remined me of Vidal Sassoon's old tagline, "If you don't look good, we don't look good." At the time, Vidal Sassoon was a company leader who believed that no matter who you were, you had a right to look your best, and they created offerings to help you accomplish that goal. That resonant tagline and the philosophy that inspired it disappeared after the company was sold to a soulless corporation with the purpose of selling hair products.

Consider the businesses you patronize most frequently. Why do you choose them? Why are they so compelling? Do you feel you are getting a special value or that they are making you feel a certain way? Do you feel they have somehow connected with what you believe? Using Apple as an example, Sinek says they are a computer company just like other computer companies. But what makes them such a powerful force is their core belief that in everything they do they want to challenge the status quo. They want their people to "think different." You don't hear them talk about power, speed, or size. In fact, their products look quite similar. Yet try to get near an Apple store on a weekend.

When we polled the leaders in our firm about companies they love, their answers ranged from Zappos to a local restaurant to Nordstrom. Interestingly, none of them mentioned their own financial advisory firm or the bank they use. Rather, they were responding viscerally about what makes them loyal to these businesses, and why they were passionate advocates for them. As one of our colleagues put it, "It's all about how they make me feel." According to Sinek, this gut decision is a giant driver of behavior that seems to defy logic, data, and facts.

But many companies are still focused on the *how* and *what*, instead of the *why* that provides a reason for these organizations' existence—or why anyone should care. In professions like financial advice, most practitioners are doing the same thing in the same way, so differentiation is hard to come by. Advisors will often claim not to have any competition, but what they never see are all the people who've opted not to call them at all.

It may be helpful to understand why prospects choose not to do business with you, or even consider your firm. What makes them pause and say, "It just doesn't feel right." If you don't know why you do what you do, how will your clients?

When we think about the many advisory firms we have visited over the years, we have vivid recollections of both the positive and negative experiences. While we weren't clients or prospects, our interactions gave us a glimpse into the first impression they make on those all-important people. There were advisors who had our names on a welcome sign, whose receptionists came around the desk to greet us warmly. Other places were well prepared to make us feel special with fresh fruit, bone china cups, and espresso machines at the ready, giving us something to enjoy while we reviewed professionally produced handouts and videos that allowed the advisors and staff to do clever presentations. In contrast, there were also firms with hovel-like offices, whose receptionists didn't know who we were or why we were there, and whose staff moped around in all forms of grumpy poses. More often than not, those were also the firms who served bad coffee in paper cups.

On reflection, it's compelling to think about the lasting impact those first impressions made on us. Clearly, the superficial elements by themselves will not engender loyalty or even passion if the rest of the firm's messaging is disconnected from the beliefs of the target client. Had we been prospects of those welcoming advisory firms, we would still want to find a connection at an even deeper level.

One of the most telling comments in a study we did several years ago about women and investing was: "My advisor does not make me feel smarter. He doesn't teach me anything. He talks down to me." No wonder the statistics show a tendency for female clients to leave their advisor after their husbands croak. The conclusion is that many advisors never felt that their purpose was to help their clients be financially literate, better informed, or more in control of the decisions they had to make.

A good example of a firm that is connected to the *why* is Personal Capital, a digital advisory firm that crossed $2 billion in assets under management (AUM) in less than four years. The company's CEO, Bill Harris, believes the core of their business is simplifying financial lives through technology and people. Allowing clients to be in control of the communication with their advisor indicates that they are also in control of their financial destiny. If they want to connect through FaceTime at 8:00 PM, that's not a problem. How about a monthly Skype session? E-mail? Chat? Phone? Okay, okay, okay, okay. The client dictates the terms of communication because Personal Capital believes that interaction with one's advisor is at its best when it accommodates each client's preferences and schedule.

Advisors who connect to their *why* are those who can articulate their purpose clearly. For example, they may express their mission as one of helping individuals to make an impact with their investments, to build wealth to spread wealth, or to help people take control of their personal financial lives.

When Michael Gerber wrote *The E-Myth* about how entrepreneurs not only survive but thrive, he made it clear that very few successful business owners were driven by the desire to own or operate a company. Most times, they started because they had an idea that could change the world, enhance the lives of others, or tap into their passion. Not one of the successful entrepreneurs whom he interviewed said their motive for starting a business was to make a lot of money.

For advisors, there are many great drivers to latch on to, but perhaps the most profound is the opportunity to affect the lives of others. Now is your chance to translate why you do what you do into a compelling draw for both employees and clients, in a way that truly separates your firm from every other financial solution provider.

Vision, Mission, Goals, Objectives

Once owners of advisory firms have developed a deep and cogent expression of their *why*, they must develop a process for turning this purpose into strategy and action. The best-managed firms demonstrate strategic discipline. The need to have a framework for making decisions is especially important now when we are experiencing a rapid rate of change.

New assumptions and new challenges have emerged since you last looked at your strategic plan, and upon assessment, you may have found that not everything you set out to do in the current plan was completed. Additionally, competitors may have introduced new innovations or tactics that could threaten your business and new opportunities have likely emerged.

For financial advisors, it's easy to assume that the business is much simpler and not much has changed over the course of a year. But experience tells us this is delusional thinking. On the one hand, if your practice is one that is not growing or evolving, chances are the seeds of destruction were planted long ago. On the other hand, if your business has been going through dynamic change, including rapid growth, the risks to your business could be growing exponentially as well. It's possible your efforts to get bigger may have caused you to miss new opportunities. It is even more common that pursuit of new opportunities may have inadvertently caused you to alter your strategic course without you even realizing it.

Key to reviewing the basics is to remind yourself of the framework you created for making strategic decisions in the first place. In other words, what's your vision for what you want your business to become? Did the choices you make throughout the year move you closer to your vision or detract from it?

For example, assume your stated long-term vision was that you wanted your firm to be recognized as the leading provider of comprehensive wealth management to business owners in your region. But most of your growth this past year came from a jump in assets from foundations and retirement plans, so much so that you hired two people to support this activity. Would you say that your investment in the business and your deployment of resources moved you closer to your vision or detracted from it? Furthermore, would you say that this dramatic growth may have even changed the strategic direction of your business?

Many advisors would argue, "Who cares? We grew revenue and we have more assets. Does it really matter where it came from?" If you measure success in short-term movement, it probably doesn't matter. But if you developed your vision and strategy thoughtfully, based on a reasonable set of assumptions, then your active pursuit of non-core business is like violating the guidelines of your investment policy statement. If you made the same type of opportunistic decision with client money after agreeing to a strategy, how would you justify it?

Now one thing we are certain about is that entrepreneurs, including financial advisors, tend to recoil whenever they hear consultant speak that includes words like *vision, mission,* and *culture.* As a result, many firms tend to avoid the time-consuming process of strategic planning and the discipline to implement it effectively. Rather, they deal with issues as they arise. That's just like your clients who want you to implement an investment strategy without going through the process of goal setting or assessment of risk tolerance. The reality is that it takes just as much effort to tread water as it does to execute a business strategy, so why not do the latter.

A Refresher

In its simplest form, a well-conceived strategic plan has four stages:

1. Strategic plan: the process through which you create a vision for what you want your business to become.

2. Focus: whereby you develop a mission statement that clearly and succinctly articulates what your firm does for whom and how you distinguish your business from others.

3. Assessment: the process by which you determine strengths, weaknesses, opportunities, and threats in light of your vision, and then create specific long-term goals for your firm.

4. Operating plan: wherein you create specific, measurable, actionable objectives to be accomplished in the next 12 months.

It is important to grasp the distinction between strategic and operational planning. The strategic plan tells you where you want to go, whereas the operating plan tells you how to get there. The tactical elements of an operating plan have immediate appeal to entrepreneurs because its action orientation is designed to create an immediate impact, like reducing costs, driving revenue, or increasing profits. When operating plans are created without the context of strategy, focus, and assessment, however, the result is often muddled and resources are poorly allocated.

Once your plan is in place, it is necessary to have a process for measuring and monitoring your progress against the plan. This step is often missed, which is why so many plans sit on the shelf gathering dust.

Where to Go from Here?

The business challenge then is to decide which phase you are in. Is it time to refresh your strategy or merely a time to assess your gaps vis-à-vis the market and the competition? At a minimum, it is a time to update the plan of action for the next 12 months. What is critical is that the action plan—your specific objectives—are specific and measurable and support one of the goals you established in your strategy.

For example, you may have five goals that sound something like this:

1. Increase the amount of revenue from our optimal client (as defined in your vision statement).

2. Increase the number of partner candidates inside our firm.

3. Improve our profit margins.

4. Add more clients that increase the average net worth of those we serve.

5. Enhance the risk management processes within our firm.

All of these are priorities for your business and each of them will require attention in the coming year. When you create an action plan for the next

12 months, if you come up with an initiative that doesn't help you move closer to any of these goals, then you should discard it. But be careful! You could easily rationalize the goal of improving profit margins without regard to which types of clients you take on board. You need to test your decisions here to make sure that if you take steps to do one thing that it doesn't compromise another. For example, improving profit margins without regard to whom you do business with could undermine your strategy and force you to misallocate precious resources.

Strategy is not marketing. Marketing is a component of one's strategy. Strategy is the sum of all your decisions that make up your business from how you structure the business, to whom you hire as employees, to what lines of business you offer, to which markets you serve. The development and implementation of a strategic plan is all about resource allocation. So if your vision is to be recognized as the leading provider of wealth management solutions for business owners in your region, then you have a framework for where you will spend your time, money, management, and energy.

The goals that you commit to then guide you to build an operating plan that helps you capture the right kinds of clients, develop your staff, improve your profitability, enhance your productivity, and protect your firm from damage. A vision for your business that will attract new business, energize you and your staff, differentiate you in the marketplace, and produce a reasonable return is the key to transforming from practitioner to business owner.

Zoom Out and Zoom In

Many businesses are created by accident without a conscious strategy. But as they evolve through their life cycles and more people become dependent on them for products, services, and paychecks, their need to develop a conscious plan becomes more important. This is especially true in the business of financial advice, in which practitioners often use the same language as everybody else to articulate their vision and "unique" proposition.

As described earlier, conventional wisdom is to create a strategy for your business that covers the next five years, and then write an operational or tactical plan that focuses on implementation for the near term, typically one year. The challenge with this approach is that assumptions change faster than your ability to execute them. Much like a suntan, you develop a nice glow for a short while and you then quickly go pale.

So for your strategic plan to work effectively, it is important to implement a process that allows you to be more nimble in periods of rapid change.

Momentum has proven to be a great force multiplier when circumstances are changing rapidly.

On several occasions, we have had the opportunity to listen to John Hagel III, cochairman of the Deloitte LLP's Center for the Edge, who challenged this conventional approach to strategic planning. John has spent the past 25 years in Silicon Valley as a successful entrepreneur and consultant, and he has a giant list of accomplishments easily discoverable online.

John argues that the most effective strategies implemented by the best-performing companies—especially in the technology arena—deploy an approach he refers to as "Zoom Out/Zoom In." The basic concept is that businesses will benefit when their leaders answer two critical questions and develop "an explicit view" of what the future market will look like. His questions are: "What will our market look like 10-20 years from now? And what kind of company will we need to be 10-20 years from now in order to be successful in that kind of market?"

With the answers to these questions in hand, leaders are able to zoom in to a very short period of time—six to 12 months—to focus on two or three initiatives that he calls "needle movers." The idea is to accelerate movement toward the longer-term direction.

The challenge with most businesses, he points out, is that they are usually spreading too few resources around too many choices, thereby not affecting any one of them. Accomplishing each of the short-term objectives helps to fund the long-term plan.

But the idea of staying actively engaged around the long-term assumptions is also important because change is a constant. He says that most companies get locked into their long-range plan and do not revisit or challenge their assumptions, and therefore don't alter their plans. Two examples of this are Kodak and Microsoft, both of which were dominant companies in their markets at one time.

Kodak, he explained, was run by chemists who believed the future of photography would always be in film. Oddly, they were among the first to have a patent on digital photography but they could not get past their bias as chemists to think the way in which pictures were processed would remain relatively constant.

Another prominent example is Microsoft, which felt the need to be the leader in desktop computing, and in fact accomplished that goal. In the beginning, this was a great perspective that gave them focus and allowed them to become dominant in computer operating systems. But as they entered into scores of new business ventures and concentrated their resource development on software applications for the desktop, they became outmaneuvered in the personal technology space by the likes of Apple and Google. In other words, they were excellent at zooming in but lost their ability to zoom out in a way that would help them challenge their assumptions, revisit their long-range vision, and make short-term decisions that would move them closer to the right long-range goal.

Hagel says it is important in this environment to get to critical mass in your market before anybody else. He noted that fast followers are rare and that it is hard to overcome the dominant provider. While the concept may not be immediately apparent to financial advisors, think about how you could localize this concept by created a winning strategy for a key client strategy in your defined market that would not be easily replicated by any other firm. For example, the strategy could revolve around a well-defined market niche, a unique solution to solve the optimal client's biggest challenge, or a recruiting program that makes your firm the employer of choice for top-performing financial advisors.

Hagel says that most companies can be categorized as one of three: (1) infrastructure management, (2) innovative product development, or (3) customer centric, meaning providing helpful solutions to consumers. He says the worst performers are those who can't decide which business they are in so they straddle all three. Hagel's advice: "Unbundle the company. Pick one and be superior. Get out of the businesses you shouldn't be in."

In financial services, an example could be a firm that manufactures and distributes mutual funds, acts as a custodian or broker/dealer, and has a direct retail business. Or an advisor who has a retirement plan record-keeping business, mutual funds actively managed by them, and a high net worth wealth management practice.

There are countless other examples but the point is that too much diversification of a business, especially into non-compatible or competing activities, tends to strain resources and retard growth in each of their lines of business. If it takes too long to explain the whole enterprise or even diagram the sentence that describes your business, you probably are badly structured.

Hagel's comments got us thinking about the many advisory firms we have encountered over the years. The best-performing firms were able to define their optimal client, think in the long term about what those clients will need and should expect from their advisor, and methodically build an offering to respond to that need. Furthermore, they were very attentive to which of those offerings they would own and invest in and which they would rent or collaborate on with other providers. For example, members of M Financial are all high-end estate planning insurance professionals who share a common resource to deliver risk-based financial solutions for complex and high-end estate planning. Individually, they don't manufacture anything, but collectively, they leverage each other's expertise as well as the balance sheet and tools of M Financial itself.

The key to an effective Zoom Out/Zoom In strategy is to constantly challenge and inform your assumptions about the business. In this industry, that would include discussions about the impact of regulation, demographics, new methods of competition, investment environment, and emerging client needs. Hagel advises business leaders to take the time to discuss long-view issues in every management meeting, and dive deeper into the issues every six months.

The second key is to think in terms of a six- to 12-month tactical plan around one to three initiatives. Hagel says, "Go fast in short increments."

Hagel points out that there are two most common failure points:

• You ignore the long term and just focus on the incremental.
• The true believer mindset in which you have a long view that is in stone.

To effectively execute a Zoom Out/Zoom In strategy, it is important to be informed by the facts. The tendency is for businesses to look at financial metrics that are interesting lagging indicators but may not be helpful in understanding trends that could affect you in the long term. The key, Hagel says, is to develop metrics that serve as leading indicators. Examples would include client satisfaction, client turnover, demonstrations of loyalty through referrals, and major sources of business opportunities among many.

The best-performing firms make the discussion around business assumptions a critical part of their regular management meetings and a key way to create ownership in the outcome that you and the rest of your team envision. An effective way to organize this discussion is to look at the trends revealed through the leading indicators. Debate what you believe the implications to be and let that help you inform the direction your business should take and the immediate steps needed to get you on the right path.

Clients of the Future

We spend a lot of time thinking about what will drive success in the future of this business. We know from financial performance studies, for example, that advisory practices are better managed today than they were just a decade ago. We also know they are larger, often more sophisticated, more independent, and more reliant on technology. Yet, something has been nagging at us about the way in which most advisory firms are oriented.

The epiphany came when we realized our view was more about the advisor of the future than the client of the future.

It seems the average advisory practice model has been built around the Baby Boom. The trade press and industry advertisements often state that retirement needs should be the focus of one's practice, especially if your market is the mass affluent. While the new liquidity created by those born after World War II is substantial, it's also clear that the wealth of this generation is more in the de-accumulation phase than in the growth phase. In other words, what is becoming available for advisors to manage and charge for are assets that were previously tied up in some other form such as a small business or a 401(k) plan. Now they are being repurposed to fund one's retirement with the hope that the last check gets paid to the funeral home. . . . And it bounces.

Retirees and pre-retirees can be a great catalyst for advisors building assets under management, but it also puts a substantial brake on how the advisory firm will grow organically.

Two commonly suggested statistics support this argument. First, real rates of return on client portfolios for the foreseeable future are estimated by many to be closer to 4 percent. And the required withdrawal rates for people financing their life in retirement will likely need to exceed 4 percent on average. We will defer to the financial planners whether they feel these rates are within the realm of reason, but few will argue that we are now in an environment in which our assumptions about returns are lower than before and our assumptions about adequate withdrawal rates are higher than previously thought.

Meanwhile, advisors whose incomes are tied to fees based on assets under management could be stuck in neutral or even face decline. Furthermore, the cost of doing business continues to rise, which will squeeze their profit margins and depress their business value.

The resulting pressure is to find more clients with newly liquid assets to offset the withdrawal rates of clients seeking to fund their lifestyle in retirement.

This has not always been the case, of course. While retirement was on the horizon, advisor growth was coming from inflows of assets and market appreciation from this group. For years, advisors could rely on the Boomers as the most important demographic from an economic standpoint that they would ever see. Heck, most advisors are Boomers, so they could relate intimately to their clients' issues. But if you viewed your client base as a laddered portfolio, you might see that you are layered too heavily in a category that will reach maturity earlier than you may desire.

To help advisors diversify their practices to include Gen X, Y, and Z, Cam Marston of Generational Insights wrote a helpful e-book titled *The Gen-Savvy*

Financial Advisor (2013 Generational Insights). Boomers were born between 1946 and 1964; Gen X clients were born between 1965 and 1979; millennials were born 1980 to 2000.

Marston's central thesis is that everyone sees the world through his or her own generational filter. While in some cases the differences between generations are minor because of things like religion or where one grew up, in many other cases, the differences are vast and consequently challenging for advisors.

While Marston acknowledges the staying power of the Boomer generation, he urges advisors to consider what they are missing by not retooling to capture their clients' children and their children's children. For example, he notes that:

- 29 percent of wealth investors are under age 50 and control 37 percent of potential investment assets.
- Investors between ages 18 and 50 will inherit more than $41 trillion by 2052.
- 86 percent of heirs say they will not use their parents' advisors.

But the book does not say all is lost. In fact, it goes through a helpful process of identifying the financial traits of each generation, ways in which to connect with members of each generation, and methods to position your business to serve the generations you are most interested in reaching.

For example, Marston identifies the millennial investor as generally well-educated—perhaps the most educated generation in history. They also tend to delay marriage, childbirth, and other adult markers until later. Of course, they grew up with technology unlike previous generations, and they tend to be both individualistic and group-oriented, a contrast that is helpful to understand. Unlike the Gen X investors before them who may be the most cynical of all generations, Millennials tend to be optimistic.

A trait common with members of the millennial generation is that they tend to be friends with their parents, which few Boomers can relate to. The positive result is that they tend to treat people from all generations as equals. Significant for advisors who may think they know all the answers and demonstrate impatience with those who don't respond to their recommendations, these new clients are not accustomed to being spoken down to. When making big financial decisions, they will likely consult with their parents and perhaps even bring them along.

Marston has contributed much to the discussion around generational differences that advisors and financial services organizations have come to appreciate. With this book, he is both challenging and instructive to advisors who are beginning to think about how they will build a business that will endure beyond them while staying relevant to clients who need their help today. The question is whether you should care.

You should care if you want to create opportunities for your partners and employees, or if you want to build a business with transferable value. You should care if you want to invest in your growth rather than simply focus on harvesting what seeds you've already sown. You should care if you are experiencing attrition through death or the retirements of your existing clients. The challenge now is how to make that change.

The answer usually begins by asking whether your strategy is still relevant. This means, do you have a clear idea of what you'd like your business to look like five or 10 years from now? Do you know who your clients are likely to be and who will be working in your practice? Do you know who will be leading it and how the business will be positioned in the market? Do you have a sense of who your competitors might be and how you will differentiate yourself from them?

Once you have framed your vision of the future including who will be your optimal client and what will be your optimal client experience, it will become more obvious as to what your organizational structure should be and what type of people you'll want to have working in your business.

For example, assuming you deem it critical to appeal to millennials, will you need to actively develop millennials as advisors who will serve them? What kind of training gap for you and them does that present? What types of tools and technology will they need to communicate with clients and make your business accessible to them?

Historically, this is a business that has made a gradual transition through the life cycle. But the generational differences present a form of revolution rather than an evolution. Different people serving different clients in different ways dictate change.

How exciting and hopeful is it that the economy is experiencing a new wave of liquid wealth, and those who are well positioned to capture this trend will also ensure a business that will last beyond them.

PART II

The Role of Demographics and the Ability to Grow

CHAPTER 3

A New Paradigm for Relating and Growing Relationships

Luck is what happens when preparation meets opportunity.

—Seneca

Seneca reminds us that we make our own luck—and today's financial services industry offers many favorable conditions to create positive outcomes for our businesses and our clients' lives. Two demographics in particular—investors under 45 and women—are quickly becoming our country's fastest wealth creators while simultaneously poised to receive the bulk of a $40 trillion wealth transfer that actually ends up in the hands of inheritors.[1]

Headlines and platitudes everywhere acknowledge the importance of these two groups, but studies continue to show that systematic, successful engagement and high satisfaction among them remains rare.

Investors under 40 and women continually report the highest levels of dissatisfaction and trust in their experience with financial services.

It is puzzling why more advisors have not yet adapted their business models to more thoughtfully serve these clients. It is especially puzzling when

---

[1] Cam Marston, "Great Wealth Transfer Will Be $30 Trillion—Yes, That's Trillion with a T," CNBC.com, July 22, 2014. Available at: www.cnbc.com/id/101751416.

you consider how challenged the typical advisory firm is to achieve its growth goals. The 2015 *Investment News* Compensation and Staffing Study[2] confirmed that this is a great business to be in with the industry overall doubling in size in the past five years.

It also found that advisory firms plan to keep this momentum with the majority aiming to grow their firm's assets under management by at least 10 percent from new business development each year.

While we are optimistic about an advisor's ability to continue to experience this kind of positive momentum and grow, their strategies need to adapt. It used to be that a 10 percent growth rate was easy to achieve by simply receiving the referrals of satisfied existing clients and relying on the personal networks of their founders. The industry, however, is changing. Many potential clients already have an advisor and are satisfied with the services they receive. Traditional brokerage firms have successfully converted their services to planning and wealth management. Many local markets are saturated with well-known advisors. The founders of advisory firms, who used to develop most of the new business, are also finding that they have tapped out the potential of their networks. The next generation of advisors has often received little or no training in how to approach new clients.

This is why we believe that it is important for every firm to change its approach to new clients and particularly find a way to reach clients they may not have approached before—younger people and women.

Table 3.1 that follows gives us a detailed look at the growth rates and some challenges by firm type. Solo firms grew by 22.4 percent compared to ensembles at 14.6 percent, enterprise ensembles at 10.8 percent, and super ensembles at 8.5 percent.

There's an anomaly in the 2015 data set that shows the fastest growth rate being achieved by the solo firms. We talked to the study's author, Philip Palaveev, who suggested that solo firms may be getting a boost as the denominator of the calculation (current AUM) favors smaller firms. The addition of $10 million in new AUM may represent 10 percent growth versus a large $1 billion firm that adds the same AUM growth adds only 1 percent growth.

But it is the larger ensemble and super ensemble firms that have and will continue to have many more advantages than smaller ones.

---

[2] *Investment News*, "The 2015 Investment News Compensation and Staffing Study," October 18, 2015. Available at: www.investmentnews.com/section/specialreport/20151018/COMPSTAFF.

TABLE 3.1　Growth Rates by Firm Type

New assets from new clients	9.9%	11.8%	6.3%	7.7%
New assets from client referrals	4.3%	4.4%	1.9%	1.5%
New assets from professional referrals	2.2%	3.7%	1.3%	1.4%
New assets from firm business development	3.4%	3.7%	3.1%	4.8%
New assets from existing clients	10.6%	2.9%	5.3%	5.2%
Lost assets from lost clients	–1.7%	–1.8%	–2.0%	–2.7%
Lost assets from existing clients	–2.0%	–2.2%	–2.1%	–5.8%
Change due to performance	5.4%	3.9%	3.4%	4.1%
Net change	**22.4%**	**14.6%**	**10.8%**	**8.5%**

These firms are more productive and more profitable than their smaller counterparts. Larger firms are able to attract larger and higher quality client relationships. They attract the best talent by offering access to work with the best clients, more development opportunities, and higher salaries.

The size of the ensemble and super ensemble firms also increases their reputation and prominence in the marketplace. In fact, investors in the study describe these firms as safer or more prestigious.

With all these tailwinds to give their strategy a lift, it's important that these firms do not get complacent. One of the best suggestions we have to prevent complacency is for firms to commit not to growth, but to *managed growth*.

We define managed growth as:

- Being committed to your culture and your clients.
- Knowing that growth at all costs is not success. Growth isn't good if you lose your soul or control of your business in the process.
- Staying true to your value proposition, business development activities, client experience, and brand—do not dilute them.
- Managing risk. It means we continue to discern the quality of the clients, employees, and partners we associate with, recognizing that one bad apple can ruin the tree.
- Never acquiescing leadership, and inspiring it at every level.

The firms that are most at risk to missing their growth objectives seem to be the ones without a disciplined commitment to managed growth.

For example, in some of the larger firms we work with we see a growing distance between the firm's clients and the firms' management team. This comes to light in examples like these:

- As firms grow and hire more relationship managers, the CEO and founding partners tend to spend more time managing and less time in client meetings. When the leadership team is removed from the client experience, yet is still responsible for the key decisions that affect clients, we start to see that the decisions they make may not be the right ones or the most relevant ones.
- Another issue we see as firms grow larger is that they become very good at client retention, but they do not invest as much in developing a business development muscle. These firms may have hired many relationship managers to manage existing clients but fail to transfer their knowledge of how to develop business to the next generation.

So how can we continue to professionally manage and institutionalize our businesses without losing touch with our clients and finding new ways to delight them with the kind of personalized service experiences today's clients expect?

Get to Know Your Ideal Client, Again

This is where understanding demographics and the changing face of wealth can play a big role. Today, many firms are too locked in to an "ideal client" type. These firms see customization and any process exceptions as an expensive endeavor, and the client asking for the accommodation, as an outlier. This can leave many clients feeling dissatisfied with a service experience that feels less than personal and unique. Silicon Valley has changed the client expectations for good with the promise of frictionless, innovative, and smart, client experiences. This kind of service experience has become long established in so many aspects of our clients' lives and the starting point for how they will define good service with today's advisory businesses.

After all, our clients are people who regularly experience extraordinary service in so many aspects of their lives, from hailing a ride to conducting online banking or personalizing purchases. Our clients expect the same consumer-grade experiences when they interact with their financial services provider. But what we find are too many who are tired, frustrated, and struggle to understand why our industry can't seem to catch up.

Financial advisory firms cannot expect to have highly satisfied and engaged clients if the service experience working with their firm does not resemble the easy and personal experiences that are so common in our everyday lives. This is a blind spot many firms have when assessing their ability to grow. This is particularly acute when we recognize that the expectations of the next generation are unforgiving of a service experience that is anything less than simple, smooth, and fun. Emphasizing and designing a client experience that satisfies the high demands of the next generation client is the fuel an advisor's business needs to gain these clients and remain a lasting and profitable business.

It's an easy argument to make, but a difficult proposition for most firms to undertake. To modernize the client experience, firms need to invest in digitizing key activities, training staff to understand the needs of each individual client and topics like unconscious bias, and modernizing office and meeting space. These are expensive and time-consuming tasks.

Many of the advisors we talk to see the need, but the payoff feels uncertain. They ask questions like, "What if I alienate my core, older clientele? How can I justify redesigning my business for clients who are not yet profitable to serve even in my current business model?"

Financial technology firms sense this hesitancy and are capitalizing on it, and they have an advantage. Without a bias toward a certain clientele or way of doing business, and without legacy processes and systems to maintain, smaller or new firms can design a business and operate with a clean slate. Without the constraints of managing an existing business, they can identify and develop a value proposition around percolating needs—the outliers or growing and new client requests—which many legacy and larger businesses have a tendency to overlook or minimize their importance as a driver of client satisfaction.

Examples of meeting these pent-up demands from potential clients may be finding a cost-effective or low-cost investing platform with instant communications for price-sensitive younger investors, or meeting their need for stability more than performance and who desire more sustainable and responsible investments in their portfolios. For female executives, it could be finding a way to deliver on the promise of a simplified service experience.

For example, a Pershing study, *The 30% Solution, Growing Your Business by Winning and Keeping Women Advisors*,[3] underscores this. It found that as Boomers retire and spend down their assets, advisors must look to the next generation of clients to take their place.

---

[3] Pershing LLC, "The 30% Solution, Growing Your Business by Winning and Keeping Women Advisors," 2013. Available at: https://www.pershing.com/our-thinking/thought-leadership/the-30-percent-solution.

The study showed that established firms seem to gravitate to investors who have already "arrived." Many women lead businesses that are smaller and newer than those owned by their male counterparts and have a knack for building successful business relationships with clients who may start off with lower asset levels but have high future potential.

These women-led smaller firms who joined the wealth management profession later, often found it easier to serve the up-and-coming client, for example: other women, younger investors, and LGBT (lesbian, gay, bisexual, transgender).

Seek First to Understand

Another reason why we see larger, established firms struggle to retain their existing clients may be a more subtle one. It's widely noted that the majority of investors cite "not feeling understood"[4] as a top reason to sever their relationship with their advisor. These investors wish for more and frequent communication and to feel appreciated.

In our work studying the generations of investors, we have found that feeling understood is deeper than the need for more communications. In relationships that are lasting and successful, there is a consistent feeling of goodwill between both parties. Investors tend to say things like, "My advisor really gets me," "I just like him," "I trust her," and "I feel safe."

The feeling is elusive. It's like charisma—hard to describe, but you know it when you see it. We call it a likability quotient and we believe it is the basis for trust, for referrals, for smooth client interactions, and for more understanding clients when things go wrong. It's critical for relationships to last.

One of the best ways to develop your likability quotient is to find and focus on the areas of common ground that you share with a client. Try to identify and amplify:

- Common interests
- Lifestyle experiences and preferences
- Similar family dynamics
- Professional and life experiences
- Generational points of view

When you share common ground with your clients, you have an almost-immediate advantage in serving them—and winning their hearts and minds.

---

[4] Roxanne Emmerich, "Misunderstood Clients Leave Their Financial Advisors Behind: There's Bad, Worse and Good News," *Illinois Banker* 90, no. 10 (October 2005).

When you are meeting with a new prospect or an extended family member of your primary client, these common-ground moments may not always be clear or available, but understanding and empathy are.

One way to create this kind of connection and demonstrate empathy is to try to imagine the world through another's eyes, to see where the other person is coming from. Trying to do this cold is difficult, but there are tendencies that individuals from a particular generation, gender, or lifestyle demographic may exhibit that can provide you with a starting point.

It takes a long time to get to know someone and the most intimate moments are discovered slowly and organically—and over a long period of time. While your newer relationships are developing, consider leveraging some of the well-documented tendencies among how different groups relate to the world and their financial advisor to build critical rapport and trust.

Our primary client relationships are likely as cemented as they are because we have found and shared many of these common-ground experiences. While not a substitute, letting generational and gender insights fill the void while natural connections are forming can increase your likability quotient and open many doors to the connections and experiences that become the solid foundation that lasting and deep relationships need.

It sounds easy and many advisors do not see this as an area of development. Yet, we so often hear the spouses or children of the primary client feel that an advisor's interest in them is self-interested or disingenuous. They may feel that the advisor is spending time with them to check the box or as a Plan B—a time in the future when the primary client is no longer around.

If the spouses and children of your clients are important to you, it has to be something that *they* feel. They need to know that you care to know them and are inspired to build that relationship in spite of any preexisting ones. Maya Angelou is credited with saying, *". . . People won't remember what you said or did; they will remember how you made them feel."* How can you apply this sentiment to your business? How are you making each one of your clients *feel* the depth of your concern and care? *Feel* confident that you have their best interests in mind? *Feel* that what you're building is not a next-generation retention strategy, but a meaningful relationship?

One way to assess how you're doing on this front is to quietly reflect on and examine your own biases. It takes a great deal of self-awareness to challenge your thinking and it's worth it to pause to regularly ask yourself questions like:

• How were your perceptions of the world formed?
• Could these old beliefs and experiences be influencing and informing how you see other people today? *Especially* people who are different from you, by gender, generation, and how they think?

- What assumptions might you be making about your clients' and prospects':
  - Needs, preferences, and desires?
  - Desired experience working with you?
  - Views on money?

Self-reflection is one thing. Try to go even further and ask your clients, prospects, and employees for feedback if you really want to add a rich layer of context and reflection. It's also a really wonderful way to demonstrate your open-mindedness, curiosity, and willingness to learn.

These kinds of behaviors can show how committed you are to designing a service experience with the other person in mind. It shows them that you care deeply enough to invest in that relationship as much as you may have with the traditional head of household or client. It shows the deep empathy and caring that is the glue to long-term, successful relationships.

If these more emotional arguments do not persuade you to invest more time and energy in designing the optimal client experience, then do it because it's one of your most positive paths for personal growth.

We believe that for the firms that are not as committed to reflecting on their client journey—crafting the opportunities to "surprise and delight" and remove the spots in which clients get stuck, for those advisors who wish to keep doing what's always worked, growth will become even more elusive.

Whereas reflecting and thoughtfully devising a client experience to serve the needs of all clients, particularly those traditionally ignored—women and investors under 40—such reflection has the potential to catapult an advisory business.

We understand that the task to understand and offer an exceptional and highly personalized client experience comes to us at a time when our entire industry is at an inflection point and there's already a lot of work to be done to retool an advisory business.

There are structural changes taking place and advisory firms need to respond to a myriad of changes. These include finding the right ways to consume so many technological and regulatory changes into their businesses. Facing unpredictable and volatile markets and trying to identify, take on board, and retain a top-performing team are just a few.

In spite of the effort it will take—and perhaps without an immediate payoff—we are committed to the idea that investing in the client experience is one of our industry's best opportunities to continue sustainable growth and retain our important client relationships.

The *first step* is to evolve our view of a target client from a monolithic persona that exists on a worksheet to a unique individual whose service expectations are informed by their life experiences, gender, generation, and other critical aspects of their demographic.

For decades, our profession has created a service experience that is based on a singular set of assumptions that went something like this: A man and woman meet, they get married, have children, build a life together, and retire happily ever after. The man was most often viewed as the head of household and the key decision maker. Individuals who mirrored this profile became the target client that most of our industry's legacy financial advisory businesses became so successful building their business around.

Today, however, families around the globe find themselves following a different calling as it relates to defining love and a meaningful life. The new definitions of family and our ideas for spending our lives also call for a new approach to financial planning and strategies to relate to and serve this new family dynamic. It's the new modern family.

As an industry, we are late to recognize how much the face of wealth has changed—it seemed to change right under us. Now, we need to remedy this and begin creating authentic connections that deliver the unique and personalized experience today's consumers want.

It's not only the profile of today's family that is changing; their life goals and priorities are also moving targets. The traditional markers of adulthood like marriage and home buying are delayed in favor of taking time to find oneself or just a desire to forgo retirement altogether and rewire, continuing to find meaningful ways to contribute and build a life.

Today, we know our clients and their needs are changing, but we have a limited understanding of what we need to do differently to serve them well. Our lack of understanding has us chasing stereotypes to try to evolve our businesses and remain relevant.

The new modern family is a whole new way of looking at family. We may see our new ideal client is a woman head of household who feels dismissed by her current advisor. Or a member of Generation Y or Z, the cadre of young people who represent the most educated and ethnically diverse generation our country has ever seen.[5]

And it turns out that even the clients who we have traditionally served and think we know well may have unmet needs. For example, many pre-retirees' and retirees' most overlooked planning needs are their emotional ones.

This is the time in life when many of our clients begin to contemplate some of their most difficult and permanent decisions, including health challenges, legacy, and life transition, and advisors need to tap into these needs to serve their client holistically.

---

[5] Scott Keeter and Paul Taylor, "The Millennials," Pew Research Center, December 10, 2009. Available at: www.pewresearch.org/2009/12/10/the-millennials/.

In all of these examples, our client experience needs to be regularly contemplated, fluid, and thoughtfully mapped to plan for the unique needs each client may have. Our recommendations should consider the generational and gender experiences and tendencies and should be highly personal and unique. Our client's experience with us should be an experience that only your firm and team can offer—if the client relationship is one that is being built to last.

It's not an easy task for today's advisory businesses to structure a service model and solution set that is relevant to up to five generations and all of these client types at one time. It may seem impossible to consider the preferences of each unique client and deliver on their rising expectations.

Having a background in the tendencies and preferences among the generations and gender can help, and it is something to keep in mind as you interact with each group. We have seen many times, when advisors bring the smallest amounts of this kind of awareness into their interactions, they are able to improve their ability to quickly relate to their clients—the new and the longstanding ones.

As our client rosters less and less resemble the clients who are familiar to us, having awareness and unbiased points of connection are the keys to the longevity of an advisor's business and to ensure that all of an advisor's client relationships are nurtured and thrive.

Once you have reconsidered your ideal client profile, the *next step* is to consider their preferences and the moments in life that shaped their lens of the world. The remaining chapters in this part will help you learn about and understand the drivers of each generation and consider the additional complexity and preferences of genders, certain niche groups, ethnicities, and other characteristics that are the client and people we value, and a critical source of our future growth.

CHAPTER 4

The Mature Client

The Greatest Generation: Your Mature Client

The Matures at a Glance*:
- Born between 1928 and 1945
- Share of adult population: 12%
- Share of non-Hispanic white population: 79%
- Political affiliation: 34% Democrat; 29% Republican; 32% Independent
- Character traits: leaders, patriarchal, conservative, value conformity, no nonsense[†]

Top concerns for advisors to address:
- **Add value in new ways.** It is long understood that traditional value propositions are waning. A mistake many make is attributing new and higher client expectations only to Millennials. Your Mature clients may be those influential in the evolution of your business and the first to demand services beyond investment expertise. Be sure to recognize that this client segment needs less of your help managing their investments and more of your help managing their lives. The aging process can be lonely and scary. Mature clients are the most

---

[*]Pew Research Center, "Millennials in Adulthood: Generations Defined," March 5, 2014. Available at: www.pewsocialtrends.org/2014/03/07/millennials-in-adulthood/sdt-next-america -03-07-2014-0-06/.

[†]Value Options, "Meet the Multigenerational Workforce," Beacon Health Options, September 5, 2012. Available at: www.valueoptions.com/spotlight_YIW/workforce.htm.

(Continued)

(*Continued*)

vulnerable for fraud or diminishing faculties—and you are in a unique role to notice and advocate for them should any of these unfortunate circumstances surface. By educating your staff on the warning signs and how to support these clients, you create priceless value and gain deep personal satisfaction for yourself knowing you've done your best to care for these clients.

- **Help them rethink risk.** Your Mature clients may become more and sometimes unnecessarily risk-averse as they contemplate a fixed-income lifestyle. You can add value to these relationships by helping them to separate emotional fears from poor decision making and help them avoid poor outcomes. Help your clients establish a strong approach to risk management, one that balances a fixed income and diminished wealth-creating potential with longer life spans, increased cost of living, and the desire for potentially more expensive aging solutions, for example, staying in one's home with full-time assistance.

The Matures (born 1928 to 1945) are roughly 20 million adults over age 70. They are an educated and wealthy generation. This generation followed the rules, married young, bought houses, raised children, and experienced professional success that was practically guaranteed. Their good fortune has not wavered. Matures hold three-quarters of America's wealth and even today continue in leadership roles of some of the most prominent companies in the country.[1]

In 2010, for the first time, the median net worth of households age 75 + ($228,400) was higher than that of *any* younger age bracket. That is more than five times higher than the median net worth of households age 35 to 44 ($44,600).[2]

This generation may be patriarchal and distant by their nature, but they are deeply engaged in intergenerational issues with their families. They are the anchor in the new modern families. They fund college educations, establish trusts, and pay for vacations. They are caregivers and 1 in 10 grandchildren lives at home with a Mature.[3]

---

[1] Value Options, "Meet the Multigenerational Workforce," Beacon Health Options, September 5, 2012. Available at: www.valueoptions.com/spotlight_YIW/workforce.htm.

[2] Neil Howe, "The Silent Generation, 'The Lucky Few' (Part 3 of 7)," Forbes.com, August 13, 2014. Available at: www.forbes.com/sites/neilhowe/2014/08/13/the-silent-generation-the-lucky-few-part-3-of-7.

[3] Ann Brenoff, "Pew Study: One in 10 Grandchildren Lives with Grandparents," *Huffington Post*, September 4, 2013. Available at: www.huffingtonpost.com/2013/09/04/grandparents-raising grandchildren_n_3866302.html.

The straightforward path to success the Matures experienced seems grown over, leaving this generation puzzled and concerned for the generations who follow them.

The Matures are children of war, either their parents' or the ones they fought in themselves. They have traditional values and family experiences. Men mostly worked and women mostly stayed home to raise the family. Today, they have tremendous influence as America's largest voting population and lead the largest lobbyist group, the AARP.[4]

They tend to be conservative and value conformity and no-nonsense approaches to most things in life. This generation lived a "waste not, want not philosophy" with noble ideas and sacrifices. Financially, they strive for comfort, security, and simplicity.

Generation Smarts: Working with Mature Clients

After years of guiding their wealth accumulation, the majority of financial institutions and advisors are highly focused on helping Matures navigate a successful retirement. Their values, plus the financial opportunity that the Matures represent, informed the wealth management experience that has been prominent for decades. Financial services firms continue to greet this generation with mahogany desks, plaques of success, and a workforce that largely mirrors the typical client: a mostly male head of household, decision maker, and wealth creator.

Financial advice for this generation tends to be communicated in the traditional advisor-client, face-to-face manner. While many members of this generation keep up with their grandchildren on social media, communication is still appreciated in person and by phone; eye contact and handshakes matter. For Matures, your reputation means everything, and financial services firms and advisors have capitalized on reputation and referrals as a key driver of business growth.

While the rules of the road were clear during the first part of their lives, navigating retirement is proving to be something different. Today's retirees face many challenges, among them living longer, changing Social Security rules, a decline in traditional defined benefit plans, and an intrinsic desire to continue to make a contribution to their communities and feel a strong sense of purpose in their lives.

---

[4] Cam Marston, *The Gen-Savvy Financial Advisor* (Mobile, AL: Generational Insights, 2013).

These shifts have many implications, and advisors must learn new dimensions for successful planning, including understanding and managing new levels of risk resulting from longevity and related expenses, including health care and helping clients retain a sense of purpose in their lives relating to their work and their causes. Keep these points in mind when engaging with a client of the Mature Generation.

Understand older clients' unique relationship with risk. The thought that goes through most of our heads when we think about giving up our income, voluntary or involuntary, are questions like:

- Will I be all right?
- Can I maintain my lifestyle?
- How can I plan for the things that I cannot plan for, like health care and life span?

These questions and concerns are especially true of older clients nearing or starting retirement. Your clients may have a tendency to become more risk-averse as they contemplate a fixed-income lifestyle. However, it is important to work with your clients to help separate their emotional insecurities and fear from sound financial planning. With life spans and the cost of living increasing, there's a paradox that exists between the desire to preserve wealth and the need to manage and perhaps take more risk. This is particularly true for female clients who face many challenges, often compounding, for example: time spent in and out of the workforce, living longer, and a strong desire to financially help their children.

Communicating on these difficult issues can become more intense at this time because of the fear and insecurity associated with getting older, health issues, and giving up an income that you can control. The advisors we work with note this as one of the most complicated transitions to manage. The clients they were used to having straightforward, black-and-white conversations with about performance and their financial goals were with clients who felt confident about their futures. Now these clients lead with emotional conversations about their well-being, and need reassurance and clear thinking on difficult emotional topics.

Recognize Your Changing Role

While helping your clients build and manage their wealth was your primary responsibility for the majority of your relationship with them, your Mature clients will be the first to challenge you to redefine your role, and often into uncharted and complicated areas.

As your clients enter this phase of life, your role may start to shift from investment manager and advisor to being called on for many intimate tasks such as becoming a life proxy and communicating between children and colleagues as clients experience more freedom, traveling, and moving farther away.

Many advisors also find themselves as the first line of defense for seniors victimized by elder fraud or exploitation—sadly even from friends, caregivers, and family members. They are also among the first to see their clients' mental and physical capacity decline or struggle with illness. Many financial advisors find coping with these new clients' needs as some of the most challenging moments in their career.

Working with Mature clients and serving them well means taking the time to learn about these transitions and vulnerabilities your clients may face—and being sensitive to them. Advisors serving the Mature client may want to offer scenario planning to help them prepare for various life experiences, many of which may be unpleasant ones, like health challenges or blended family dynamics. Offering services to help your older clients plan for the outcomes they would want in these circumstances can be a valuable part of your service offering. Your team also may need training and information on how to recognize and support clients through critical moments as they age. To retain clients in this phase of life, success is more about the peace of mind you can provide much more than the alpha you may return.

Communicate with Sensitivity and Empathy

As your older clients begin to slow down—with hearing, sight, or general getting around, you may be required to reconsider how you communicate and engage with them. Andy Reder, owner and managing partner of Kistler-Tiffany Advisors, finds the transition of aging one of the most profound and challenging of his career as an advisor.

For Andy, a Baby Boomer himself, his retiree clients are clients he has worked with for 10 to 20 years. During that time, they were young and vital and Andy's responsibilities centered on the services he provided related to their financial planning and investment management needs. His conversations with his clients were largely about performance and investment choices—all things surrounding the portfolio—and how the clients were tracking their goals.

At this phase in life, reporting is much more simplistic. Older clients care much more about the safety of their assets and feeling safe overall; this becomes the center of the conversation. Clients are interested in knowing where their assets are, they want to hear about things going on in the world, and importantly, they want to know that they will be okay.

Aging is a delicate and subtle shift. It's hard to point to the day or point in time when you suddenly need to start working with your clients differently or modifying your service experience to support them.

Now, instead of presenting the financial plan, Andy finds himself having the financial conversation *and* paying extra attention to notice if his client is hearing well, how they remember a conversation, and important account information. At the first sign of a decline related to any of these, Andy and his team take action. Sometimes it means contacting children and attorneys. Other times they adapt their process to both better support the client and protect their firm.

Andy describes his retired client of 12 years, John. John retired active and healthy at 67. John is a birder, attended sporting events, and bought a second home with his wife. He has plenty of hobbies and interests and enough investment income to live comfortably while exploring them. Life was good the first 10 years of retirement and things were working out exactly as planned. Fast forward to John's late 70s and John starts to experience the first of many health issues and an overall decline. The most troublesome to Andy is in John's cognitive deficits.

This challenged Andy's firm to work differently to identify and support John and clients similar to him. For example, when making investment recommendations to clients who have memory challenges, Andy is taking the extra step of providing the recommendation in writing, e-mailing it to the client, and having the client return the e-mail or sign the document to confirm everything. He is also making sure his wife attends the investment review sessions and frequently provides home visits. The home visits originated from a small, passing comment made by their client to Andy's assistant. The 30-minute drive was beginning to feel like an inconvenience. Andy's astute team not only picked up on this new challenge, but instituted the home visits as a way to support their client and ensure there was no disruption to their client's service experience or need to remain engaged in important aspects of overseeing their wealth and financial health.

Another client of Andy's started to suffer from a deterioration in his hearing. At first, it was managed well, but the minor issues are now major ones. This became a real challenge for Andy's staff when you consider how easy it is to pick up the phone to convey quick information in between more formal account review meetings. Once again Andy met the client where he was, and now only conducts meetings in a face-to-face setting. Today, nothing is done over the phone and e-mail is used only occasionally. Andy is modeling the way for advisors who are dealing with aging clients. He is also showing deep sensitivity and a willingness to put his standard of care above personal inconvenience.

Change the Conversation

It can be confusing to advisors to see the same client whom they worked with for so many years shift not only physically, but in what is important to them. Reconsider your traditional meeting agendas. Use the time to emphasize the things that your client may really be thinking about; for example, reinforcing the custodial relationship and the strength and stability of the organization where the assets are kept is a great conversation to have with this cohort. Talk to these clients to reinforce the ways that you are monitoring their assets and that you're regularly confirming to ensure that the allocations are appropriate and comfortable.

These clients are acutely aware that what they have saved has to last. They now make choices that only a few years ago were not choices. Decisions like going out to dinner, taking a vacation, which cars to buy. Choosing what they spend their money on is now a process and focused on trade-offs. This is true even for many wealthy families, those in the $3–$20M range. They too are focused on balancing the preservation of capital with the integrity of their lifestyle.

The point is that when you work with the Mature generation, it is important to recognize that your clients have different priorities as they age. While they may not know how to articulate it, they are thinking about different things and it will be beneficial if you can shift the conversation from beating a benchmark to topics areas of focus like wealth preservation and creating comfort in the plan and achieving the clients' goals.

Train and Empower Your Sales Assistants to Look for Signs of Aging

Thinking about Andy Reder's experiences again for a moment. Andy has a trusted assistant of 20 years, Sally Polonsky. Sally knows Andy's clients as intimately as he does. She manages all of the day-to-day support for each relationship, so throughout the year, she may even have more touch points with their clients than Andy does. Many advisors have similar relationships and would benefit from training your staff on elder care issues and then checking in with them regularly.

For example, it was Sally who found herself explaining the Required Minimum Distribution (RMD) dollar amount to a client and how he took it the previous year. Sally noted how strange it was when the same client called only a short time later and needed to be walked through the calculation in the same detail again.

Sally shared this with Andy and gently with the client's spouse. Although we all have them from time to time, she documented the "senior moment." To some observers, this could seem unnecessary. After all, what if it happened only once? Keeping this kind of documentation, however, protects the advisor, and may be helpful to the client or the extended family of the client. It can provide them with a record of the transaction and should something like this become a pattern, it may also allow an opportunity for the family to learn more and if necessary, consider or receive help.

Another critical opportunity for your staff to help, and also become a very important first line of defense, is to watch for signs of elder care fraud or account fraud overall. Seniors were always vulnerable, and are even more so in the digital age.

Today, our clients tell us how common it is for their clients to make requests for funding through e-mail, particularly surrounding extraordinary, one-time large expenses like purchasing a new home or gifting to a family member or charity. Nearly every one of those clients also has told us a mirror story of how many of those clients experienced a fraudulent attempt on their account.

A story we heard recently was from an advisor who has been working with his elderly client to evaluate continuing care communities. These are facilities that older individuals or couples may consider when they're ready to or need to leave their primary residence. These communities offer many services, including tiered levels of housing (standalone homes to nursing care facilities), social services, and increasing levels of assistance as required.

After a few months of this discussion, the advisor received a request for a lump sum of money to make a deposit for housing in one of these communities. The advisor or his assistant didn't give it much of a second thought. In this relationship, after all, they frequently communicate by e-mail and the reason for the money was consistent with their discussions.

A few years ago, however, this firm tightened its policies and procedures and they now call every client who requests funding to make sure that the request is valid. It was a huge surprise and shock to both the advisor and the client to learn that this request was never made and that someone had infiltrated his e-mail. From other e-mails and requests for information, it could be discerned that the client was looking at transitional living accommodations, figured it was a likely scenario that would check out with a less sophisticated advisor, and requested a wire.

Ensuring extra training of your team and broadening their awareness on issues related to all fraud, in particular elder fraud, is prudent. It is also important to empower your team to escalate any doubts generated from actions or their intuition with you in a way that feels safe and appreciated. This is an excellent opportunity to create or improve a culture of risk management and to care for your Mature clients.

Case Study: Connecting with Pre-Retirees and Retirees

As your clients redefine retirement, so must your business, including how you approach planning for it and the solutions you offer. This self-reflection and willingness to adapt is critical to effectively serve your clients, be relevant, and meet their new needs and desires.

For example, until recently it was sufficient for a financial advisory firm to focus most often on the male head of household and offer retirement solutions that focused on portfolio management, thoughtful withdrawals, and estate planning strategies.

Today, we still need to offer and invest in these core services such as helping our clients understand the decisions and issues related to planning their estate and retirement plans, but there is more.

Jim Pratt-Heaney, one of the founders of Westport, Connecticut-based, LLBH Wealth Management, has a unique way of seeing what *really* motivates his clients and he's built a service offering around it.

A few years ago, Jim recognized that most of his pre-retiree clients were reluctant to retire and, of those who did, the most satisfied were those living out retirement, not on a yacht, but working in their second, dream career.[5]

LLBH's experience mirrors what we see across the board, with nearly 30 percent of men and women in this generational cohort finding themselves returning to full-time or nearly full-time work after fully or partially retiring.[6]

In fact, from 1985 to 2014, the rate of participation in the labor force for people 65 to 69 increased to 32 percent from 18 percent, according to Bureau of Labor statistics. And the AARP reports that adults over 75 are more likely to be in the labor force today than they were 20 to 30 years ago.[7]

---

[5] Interview with Jim Pratt-Heaney, by telephone, August 2015.

[6] Richard W. Johnson, Barbara Butrica, and Corina Mommaerts. "Work and Retirement Patterns for the G.I. Generation, Silent Generation, and Early Boomers: Thirty Years of Change," Working Paper Executive Summary. Center for Retirement Research at Boston College, July 2010. Available at: http://crr.bc.edu/wp-content/uploads/2010/07/wp_2010-8-5081.pdf.

[7] Kerry Hannon. "As Workers Delay Retirement, Some Bosses Become More Flexible," *New York Times*, August 21, 2015. Available at: www.nytimes.com/2015/08/22/your-money/delay-retirement-flexible-work-schedules.html.

Jim and his team grasped that the psyche of today's retiree was different. They recognize that today's retiree wants to feel valued, that they're contributing and making a difference. In other words, they still have a lot to share with the world and they're determined to do it.

To support their pre-retiree and retiree clients, LLBH began adding career counseling and life coach services to LLBH's client service model. The addition of these services had many benefits. It felt great to Jim and his team to support their clients as they looked to find fulfillment and purpose in their lives. Their clients responded positively too, the relationship was deepened, and new business referrals began to flow.

LLBH plans for its male clients living on average to 93 and female clients to 95 years of age. If their clients retire at 65, it's plausible to spend 30 years or more in retirement. It sounds dreamy to never have to work again, but many men and women underestimate the emotional changes that come with this life transition.

The emotional challenges we see most affecting today's retirees relate to their search for meaning and the ability to continue to make a difference. Retiring clients over 65 struggle to adapt to these emotional changes associated with the "afternoon of life." We see it materialize in many ways, including the divorce rate. In fact, for Americans 65 and older, the rate of divorce has nearly tripled (2 to 5 per 1,000).[8]

Many factors can contribute to this life questioning and the new desires of retirees, but the biggest driver we see relates to the answers many in this cohort seek: "How can I make the most of the time I have left?" and "How can I have more fun?"

LLBH sees many advisors engaging with their clients on retirement investment strategies and the more typical ancillary services such as tax, estate, and insurance solutions into their financial planning offerings. The types of questions they ask their clients and ways they engage are fairly superficial. Questions like "Is your estate in place?" or "Can we connect with your accountant?" are interesting, but they keep the conversation framed around the client's finances.

Very few advisors are asking really interesting questions, that LLBH has incorporated into all of their pre-retiree and retiree meetings, like "What are you going to do with your life?" These questions have the potential to really open up your client and take the conversation from one of finances to one of your life.

---

[8] Susan L. Brown, I-Fen Lin, and Krista K. Payne, "Age Variation in the Divorce Rate, 1990–2010," National Center for Family & Marriage Research (NCFMR), Bowling Green State University. Available at: https://www.bgsu.edu/content/dam/BGSU/college-of-arts-and-sciences/NCFMR/documents/FP/FP-12-05.pdf.

LLBH listened to their clients and responded by adding to their traditional financial planning repertoire ways to help their clients find and develop meaning in their life. They now offer services to counsel clients who are thinking of retiring about what it really means to do so. They ask the hard questions, "Will you really be traveling at 85?" "Do you really need such a big house for the two times a year your children come?"

Clients often have a vision of retirement that is largely emotional and based on what they always thought it *should* look like. During the 30 or 40 years many investors spent working, many were also dreaming about a time when they would be free to travel and see the world. Many retiring adults are fortunate to experience this kind of freedom and world traveling excursions in the early retirement years, but tend to fail to anticipate health or life challenges they may encounter as time goes on that begins to limit these plans and their desire to be away.

Many pre-retirees and retirees also feel an emotional connection to their big homes where they raised their families. These homes tend to be located in suburban locations with large yards, driveways that need shoveling, roofs to repair, and so on. The big family house is expensive to maintain and rarely are the children showing up as often as we envision. In today's world, it's the grandparents often traveling to the children and helping them to manage their lives, not the children coming home for visits.

The team at LLBH isn't afraid to pose these questions and ask their clients to dig deeper into what kind of life they envision and what they will really find satisfying and pragmatic. They find these conversations often guide their clients to new and more fulfilling versions of retirement. They often find the previous vision of retirement didn't really belong to them as much as it did to some idea of the way it ought to be.

When these retirees and pre-retirees are pushed to formulate their own visions, LLBH finds that many of their clients begin to reinvent their lives. Now, rather than having discussions about roof replacements, they're helping their clients stay engaged in their communities; they're helping to vet private equity opportunities and fund start-ups.

This tends to be good for everyone. At this phase of life, work isn't usually about paychecks and benefits. Work can now give us access to community, relationships, a sense of fulfillment, purpose, and structure.

For today's retiree, especially men, these are immeasurable benefits, when you consider how men often rely on work for their social network and how important a social network is for one's well-being.[9]

---

[9] Ben Heaven et al., "Supporting Well-Being in Retirement through Meaningful Social Roles: Systematic Review of Intervention Studies," *The Milbank Quarterly: A Multidisciplinary Journal of Population Health and Health Policy* 91, no. 2 (June 2013): 222–287. Available at: www.ncbi.nlm.nih.gov/pmc/articles/PMC3696198/.

If you don't know where to get started as you counsel your clients to help develop new interests and find opportunities, there are many outstanding organizations that can help such as Encore.org and the National and Community Service organization (www.nationalservice.gov) that help connect older adults with opportunities to contribute their expertise to community.

It's a real privilege for our clients to never have to work again, and have the opportunity and freedom to think about what they really want to do. And it has become our privilege to help them figure that out.

—Jim Pratt-Heaney

LLBH *first* stress tests their clients' portfolios with the assumption that they'll never have to earn another penny again. With this confidence intact, they introduce a new layer of planning to their retiree and pre-retiree service model.

They work with their clients to redefine their vision of retirement. If their client is considering a new business venture, they provide scenario planning to help their clients anticipate what can happen if the new venture doesn't go as planned. The team works with their clients to think through unexpected life events such as disability, the need for extended or long-term care, and tax consequences on estates after death to ensure that the portfolio can withstand a significant financial challenge and that their lifestyle is protected.

Next, the team helps their clients make the transition from work to life after work and all that it entails and is supportive of their new vision. The work LLBH has done with so many clients has given the team perspective and wisdom. They often know how to help their clients get started on their new endeavors.

There are, however, times when they do not have the exact skills to meet the needs of these mid-life transitions or, it would make their service model less productive to really dig in with the level of detail their clients need.

In these cases, LLBH taps into what they call their virtual family office. The virtual family office is a highly trusted network of experts who provide trusted and deep expertise on critical issues including employment and settlement law and complex business negotiations. This model allows LLBH to provide the services their clients need, but that they may not have or staff for internally.

The virtual family office approach allows the team at LLBH to make connections and stay involved in their client's life. It also benefits from the relationship-deepening that these services provide and creates a new referral channel between these service providers and LLBH.

Consider adding these services to your lineup. When done well, a rich network modeled after a family office can link all of a family's professional advisors together. Now, rather than operating in silos, these professionals work together to create a seamless approach to meeting the client's needs.

Here are some best practices to consider as you get started:

- Spend time to think about and thoroughly define a governance model. The team at LLBH is the facilitator or conductor of this opera, getting their clients access to the right professionals, eliminating gaps in the planning process, and really earning them the spot of trusted advisor, not only for their money management, but their life management, too.
- Create a shared client service level agreement to ensure that the high quality service your firm provides is consistently offered to and experienced by your client no matter which network-partner firm they may interact with. After all, these third parties become an extension of not only the services you offer, but also your brand, reputation, and client experience.
- Take an honest assessment of your core competencies and understand clearly where you have gaps or a part of your offering that the client would receive a better experience working with a member of the virtual family office. Typical areas of expertise that we see advisors look to tap their network for include professionals with a deep understanding of private and publicly traded investments, business interests, philanthropic structures, trust and estate plans, real estate, taxes, family dynamics and governance issues, and career and life counseling.

In the case of LLBH, their team generally plays two critical roles:

1. They act as the registered investment advisor and are responsible for developing an overall asset allocation strategy and making investment decisions on behalf of their clients.
2. They serve as the trusted advisor who "owns the relationship." You could imagine the partner in charge of the relationship to see him- or herself as the chief relationship manager to the family. At LLBH, this is a critical responsibility. This person is often one of LLBH's most experienced, and his or her work is overseen by a managing partner. They are responsible to fully understand the family's mission for their wealth, their risk temperament, and objectives, not only of the primary head of household client, but of each individual in the family.

They are skilled in coordinating the information flow among all advisors and reporting back to the family in a timely and articulate manner.

When LLBH does not have the expertise at hand, they may tap any number of partners. Some recent examples include:

• Leveraging a number of partners, including the wealth management or family office division of a major accounting firm experienced in sophisticated tax matters, project management, and consulting.
• Consulting with a boutique investment bank that is skilled in analyzing existing and future private investments to better help their client make sound decisions.
• A firm specializing in sophisticated trust and estate plan design and providing them the ability to work with their clients and give them access to legal, tax, and insurance resources.

Mastering the virtual family office has become a core differentiator and competitive advantage for LLBH. It allows them to deliver better investment, tax, legal, investment banking, and consulting services. It earns them the coveted trusted advisor, lead advisor status and it allows them to deliver on nearly every need for their clients. The virtual family office model helps LLBH succeed by offering the important money management strategies their clients require and the very valued and very intimate life management skills and resources clients want.

CHAPTER 5

The Baby Boomers

You've Come a Long Way, Baby (Boomers)

Baby Boomers at a glance*:
- Born between 1946 and 1964
- Share of adult population: 32%
- Share of non-Hispanic white population: 72%
- Political affiliation: 32% Democrat; 25% Republican; 37% Independent
- Character traits: competitive, idealistic, team players, nostalgic, proud of their country, proud of their accomplishments[†]

Top concerns for advisors to address:
- **Uncover their purpose.** Many Baby Boomers are in the fortunate position to see their work ethic pay off. They're in senior leadership roles and at the peak of their career. If they've achieved financial stability, chances are they are ready for something more: purpose. Your Baby Boomer clients will value your services more, and find your offering unique, if you can help them create a clearer line of sight between their investments and their personal values and legacy.

---

[*] Pew Research Center, "Millennials in Adulthood: Generations Defined," March 5, 2014. Available at: www.pewsocialtrends.org/2014/03/07/millennials-in-adulthood/sdt-next-america-03-07-2014-0-06/.
[†] Value Options, "Meet the Multigenerational Workforce," Beacon Health Options, September 5, 2012. Available at: www.valueoptions.com/spotlight_YIW/workforce.htm.
[‡] Greg Iacurci, "Retirement Specialists Have Outsized Influence in Advisor-Sold DC Market," *Investment News*, September 16, 2015. Available at: www.investmentnews.com/article/20150916/FREE/150919938/retirement-specialists-have-outsized-influence-in-adviser-sold-dc.

(Continued)

(Continued)

- **Provide retirement expertise.** Baby Boomer clients are in transition to either pre-retiree or retiree. The path to security and feeling good is fraught with difficult choices. The decisions range from the emotional (selling homes, ending careers, or reinventing careers) to those around investment and savings (how much is enough, strategies to catch up, Social Security, and long-term care). With less than 5 percent of advisory business specializing in retirement issues and a dire need from your clients for information, specializing in the issues surrounding retirement may be the intersection of your clients' greatest need with your greatest ability to make a difference.

The Baby Boomers are the 75 million Americans born between 1946 and 1964[1] or 28 percent of today's Americans. Whether it was their sheer size or how the world responded to them, Baby Boomers always understood their influence and they exercised it to their benefit.

Born between 1946 and 1964, the Baby Boomers get their name from the boom in the birthrate following World War II.[2] As these 75 million individuals grew up, they singlehandedly reshaped how we experienced and viewed life and society. Caught in the middle of some of the most turbulent and important moments in our history, they grew up idealistic, holding to these principles and using them to reshape how we work, how we consume and purchase. Today, they are also changing the way we age—or if we age at all!

This generation was promised the American Dream and they relentlessly pursued it. As a result, they are often viewed or experienced on two ends of a spectrum—selfish, materialistic, and ambitious, or idealistic, forever young, and collaborative. But most of all, they are optimistic, and believe without a doubt that there is no problem or challenge that cannot be solved or accomplished without hard work and a good attitude.

The Baby Boomers singlehandedly changed the way businesses operate, their preferences and values heavily influencing the marketing, sales, and service strategies of many businesses to meet their needs, appeal to their preferences, and win their business.

---

[1] Richard Fry, "Millennials Overtake Baby Boomers as America's Largest Generation," April 25, 2016. Available at: www.pewresearch.org/fact-tank/2015/01/16/this-year-millennials-will-overtake-baby-boomers/.

[2] Cam Marston, *The Gen-Savvy Financial Advisor: Advising the Generations in the New Age of Uncertainty* (Mobile, AL: Generational Insights, 2015).

The financial services industry is no exception. From mahogany desks, credentials, and degrees on display to hierarchical organizations and firm handshakes, we crafted a client experience around the Baby Boomer client. If we were to describe it, we might say built around a male archetype. It was designed to appeal to and service the face of wealth our country is most familiar with: one that tended to be the male head of household who was most often out earning the wealth and deciding where and how it might be invested.

Generation Smarts: Working with Baby Boomers

The Baby Boomers are the wealthiest generation of consumers in American history.[3] The U.S. 50-plus population spends $3.2 trillion annually. That is more than the GDP of nations such as Italy, Russia, the United Kingdom, Brazil, and France![4]

Boomers far exceed younger investors when it comes to holding financial investments by more than 50 percent over investors aged 18 to 49—and the investments that they do hold are valued 197 percent greater than those of younger investors.[5]

With so much emphasis on the next generation of investors, many advisors begin to wonder if the Boomers will still have the same clout and meaning in their business. Make no mistake: This generation is just getting started.

This demographic is living longer than any other generation in our history.[6] Our treasured industry colleague and friend, Cam Marston, is an expert on the topic of generational savviness. Marston often jokes that the Boomers are in cahoots with the pharmaceutical companies to stay alive indefinitely, and we are beginning to think he is on to something!

This "refusing to age" demographic is wiping away stereotypes and images in our mind of old age. Based on how well they're living and their continued good prospects, some researchers have called to redefine old age to

---

[3] Ibid.

[4] Mark Bradbury, "The 7 Incredible Facts about Boomers' Spending Power," *Huffington Post*, May 17, 2015. Available at: www.huffingtonpost.com/mark-bradbury/the-7-incredible-facts-about-boomers-spending_b_6815876.html.

[5] Ibid.

[6] Ibid.

be as having 15 or fewer years left to live. This means for the Baby Boomer generation, they will still be middle aged until their 74th year.[7]

It seems they've not only figured out a way to live longer, but to live really well while they're doing it. They are youthful in every sense and marketers capitalize on this. The stock photography now used to engage them on websites or in brochures is full of youthful, active, fulfilled adults—no one is sitting on a couch watching life go by.

Boomers continue to occupy the majority of senior leadership and management positions at work and are at or near their earning peak.[8] While the oldest Boomers may just be beginning to retire, the youngest are in their late 40s or early 50s and face many of the same lifestyle challenges as Generation X—raising children, working hard, building wealth—most Boomers are still making plans and have a lot of life left to live. In other words, they are still very good and relevant clients for most advisory firms.

The demographers in our industry have divided the Boomer generation into two groups: Early Boomers, born 1946–1955, and Trailing Boomers, born 1956-64.[9]

Marston's research concludes that while similar experiences and attitudes informed both groups, they are at very different life stages with different financial priorities, and advisors need to understand the distinction.

The Early Boomers are close to or have entered retirement. They have grown children and they are in transition. They are adjusting their lifestyles: selling primary residences, contemplating second homes and warm locations, and looking to their advisor for confidence that they can retire comfortably, handle unexpected expenses, and make their savings last for the 30-plus years many of them will spend in retirement.

Trailing Boomers may more closely resemble the generation who follows them, Generation X (more about this cohort soon). Many are in their prime earning years and have no plans to stop working: some because they may have children still at home and many obligations still to come; others may have experienced the burn of the financial crisis and working longer is a necessity.

Other Trailing Boomers are extending their retirement horizon for more optimistic reasons, including how much they enjoy their career and the contributions they are making at work or in their communities. This group is a spirited group. If they have any plan for life after work, it's to continue to reinvent

---

[7] Sarah Knapton, "Old Age Does Not Begin until 74, Researchers Suggest in a New Report Which Looks at the Real Impact of an Ageing Population," *The Telegraph*, April 15, 2015. Available at: www.telegraph.co.uk/news/uknews/11539573/Middle-age-now-lasts-until-74-as-baby-boomers-refuse-to-grow-old.html.

[8] See Note 4.

[9] Ibid.

themselves and find many new ways to pursue their ideals. Keep these points in mind when engaging with a client of the Baby Boomer generation.

Invest in Building Relationships—the Old-Fashioned Way

Similar to the Mature generation, the Baby Boomer cohort will feel appreciated and valued by you in proportion to the effort you put into the relationship. This generation values face time (the real thing, not the app) and tends to prefer to do business and have intimate conversations in person.

When compared to their generation peer groups, a recent study found that Generation X and Y's preference for meetings at the advisor's office was half that of Baby Boomers![10] Baby Boomers are your most likely client to make time for and appreciate spending social time together.

Depending on personal preferences, of any of the cohorts, this is the group that may be the most likely to suggest ways of combining business and pleasure. It may be on the golf course or over lunch and meetings in your or their office. The place is most often trumped by their desire to work together and communicate face to face.

Many advisors who also happen to be a part of the Boomer generation may find that working with these clients is among of their most pleasurable relationships to manage. There is often an instant sense of compatibility. Advisor and client quickly relate to the life phase the other is in; they tend to have similar goals and challenges, whether it relates to saving enough or being caught in the challenges of the sandwich generation (caring for children and parents at the same time).

When there is so much overlap in life's moments, there can be a sense of understanding that strengthens the relationship and makes building trust easier. However, when younger advisors are engaged and asked to manage a relationship with a Baby Boomer client, they can struggle in many ways to find those points of connection. One area in particular is around communication preferences.

Here are two suggestions to ease this strain.

Provide Training for Your Team

While we like to avoid generalizations, there are some tendencies that resonate more with some generations than others and these have been documented by many researchers. If you're unsure where to begin, a subject matter expert can assist you. Cam Marston, for example, provides specialized training. He

---

[10] Michael Kitces, "Best Practices in Client Communication for Financial Advisors," Nerd's Eye View at Kitces.com, March 3, 2014. Available at: https://www.kitces.com/blog/best-practices-in-client-communication-for-financial-advisors/.

is also the author of a workbook and online course, *The Gen-Savvy Financial Advisor*, which can provide quick insights that make a meaningful impact on your client experience. You can learn more about Cam's resources here: www.generationalinsights.com

A few tips to get you started:

- Baby Boomers are not afraid to question authority, so do not be surprised if this generation presses you to explain more or for details to proposals or in general during conversation. To avoid feeling like you are defending your ideas and recommendations, give your Baby Boomer clients choices and more choices, to demonstrate your flexibility. Ask them to weigh in on the options provided. Remember that this generation likes to work as a team. They will appreciate receiving options and the discussion that ensues as creating the environment of collaboration and teamwork that they thrive in.
- This generation was rewarded for and celebrates their achievements. Baby Boomers love a rich history, and your story of hard work, diplomas, and collected accolades will resonate with them. Develop a corporate narrative for your firm, present your firm's history and experience colorfully, and then pivot and frame it in a way that helps your Boomer clients see the big picture and their future. Be sure to take the time to pause and underscore how your proposal will help them achieve and celebrate their goals.
- Embrace paradoxes. For sure, there is a large part of the Baby Boomers who are intimidated by and avoid current high technology. Yet, the Baby Boomer generation spends more on technology than any other generation.[11] Do not be afraid to try social media, particularly Facebook and LinkedIn, to reach this group. Most of them have a smartphone and a tablet and many are fluent in using them to communicate.

Never Assume

The most sophisticated client communication programs have a systematic way to understand, document, and adapt to a client's communication preferences. It seems innocuous to call when your client might really prefer e-mail, yet, over time these small frictions can really negatively affect the way people relate to each other, how welcome the communications and interactions are, and ultimately become a real point of dissatisfaction in a relationship—no matter how positive the other interactions.

---

[11] H. E. James, "Baby Boomers Gain Freedom through Technology," Tech.co, July 14, 2015. Available at: http://tech.co/baby-boomers-gain-freedom-technology-2015-07.

To avoid these unnecessary frustrations, many of the advisors we work with automatically ask clients their communication process during the onboarding process and regularly throughout the relationship.

Pershing's annual *Study of Advisor Success* in 2014[12] noted that in addition to wanting to have a say in *how* they are contacted, investors also wanted a say in the *frequency* of communications.

Consistent and predictable communications can help build the foundation of trust between you and your clients. The more frequent and tailored communications between you and your client, the more your clients can understand what to expect and in general, the more satisfied your clients will feel. It's also worth noting that the study found that too many advisors have not yet invested in or developed a client-driven communications strategy. This is a missed opportunity. It is critical for advisors to understand how, where, and when current and potential clients prefer to communicate, as these seemingly small irritations can add up to be big "dissatisfiers" in a relationship. They are also the nuanced pain points that open the door to your client taking a call from another advisor.

We work with a large firm who, for a long time, had as one of their strong points their meeting follow-up. In each quarterly touch point, the advisor and his team would document the actions the client should do in the time between meetings. It could be things like talk to their attorney and finalize a trust or shop for more insurance. No matter what the issues were, the checklists and the client service representative checking in and nudging the next steps along was meaningful to many of this advisors' clients.

For a period of time, this advisor experienced some heavy turnover among some of his key account management and junior advisory staff. These staffers were the people who would ensure that these valuable communications and follow-ups happened. They misunderstood the weight his clients placed on the follow-up calls and the help they represented. The advisor stopped these communications between meetings while he managed with fewer administrative and junior staff.

The advisor thought any dissatisfaction his clients might experience as a result of the turnover was more about what they experienced during the in-office meetings and having a consistent contact person than the contact the clients placed on the communications between meetings. This advisor often

---

[12] Pershing, "The Most Successful Advisors Adapt to Client Communication Preferences, Pershing Study Says," press release, June 5, 2014. Available at: https://www.pershing.com/news/press-releases/2014/the-most-successful-advisors-adapt-to-client-communication-preferences-pershing-study-says.

extended himself to be present at the meetings and show his commitment to the relationship, but he completely missed that the driver of so much of the relationship goodwill was the communications his clients had come to rely on. He didn't understand when he lost two important clients that what opened the door to another advisor was the promise of more regular communications and help following up on all the other critical items necessary to have your financial health and life in place. As with many things in life, if we see the world only through our own filter and what we value rather than through the eyes of others, we can often miss easy opportunities to create and sustain the goodwill and ease a relationship needs to survive.

Use Straight Talk

There is much to be said about Baby Boomers and their unrelenting ties to their youth. Many communication experts would advise you to talk to them about their well-being and appeal to their agelessness. It's often recommended to speak in terms of their future, but in a way that conjures up their youth.

Let's return again to Andy Reder's practice, in which Andy counsels wealthy individuals and many Baby Boomers. All of his clients ask him to create a pro forma to estimate their living expenses and to feel confident that they can continue to live well and retire on the amount they have saved. In typical Boomer fashion, many of them do not believe they will start slowing down until age 95 or thereabouts.

What Andy has found over the years is that his Baby Boomer clients are correct. In their late 60s and early 70s, they do need a similar cash flow that they received in their pre-retirement years. These early retirement years are the years they are traveling, entertaining, and dining out as they always did. It's during these years that many of his clients also make significant gifts to their children, usually in the form of tuition or home down payments. However, what Andy sees that many of his clients fail to realize is that by the time they enter their mid to late 70s, their lifestyle drastically changes. They stop going out as much, buying new clothes is less frequent, traveling long distances starts to feel like a hassle, and all around they start spending less.

What stood out to Andy is how few advisors want to counsel them on this common tapering of activity and spending. In spite of the warnings to make Baby Boomers feel young at all costs, Andy takes the issue head on and in doing so has found his Baby Boomer clients appreciate the candor, and trust him more. They envision their retirement in new ways and while they don't front-load their expenses in the early years, they do prioritize their most meaningful dreams and moments and make sure to make time for them. Our experience with investors supports this. The more direct, the more candid, the more you can provide the breadth of your experience, the more drawn clients are to you and your advice, and the relationship overall is more sticky on account of its authenticity.

Be Helpful in New, Unexpected, and Highly Valued Ways

Many of our clients find that their older Boomer experience not only gives them more fatigue or health issues as they age, they also feel overcome by the things that once provided great pleasure, for example, travel. The same clients who were once vital, nothing is going to stop us Baby Boomers traveling every few weeks or months to all of our bucket list places, now find the activities like carrying bags and the reliance on technology for everyday tasks like printing a boarding pass or checking in to a flight to be overwhelming.

One of the advisors with whom we work recently visited his client to review the client's portfolio. The client was distracted during the meeting and confessed to not being able to concentrate on account of being worried about the details surrounding the trip he and his wife were taking the next day. The things that can feel like they're making us more efficient and that are simplifying their lives, like using the airport kiosk to print boarding passes, had this older client perplexed and stressed.

The advisor in this story pressed pause on his own agenda and what he wanted to cover with the client to call their son who lives nearby and ask him to print and bring a copy of the boarding pass to his father. This small act of solving this seemingly small problem was the highlight of our advisor's client's afternoon. The stress of traveling without feeling intimidated or unsure was relieved. While there was very little said about the investment conversation our advisor had planned, he was far from frustrated. Rather, the advisor found the entire experience rewarding because he was able to help his client and the client was appreciative.

This story seems simple but for us it was powerful because it framed value in a new way. This older Boomer client who was starting to feel a little intimidated about the world was now very appreciative. As the advisor was leaving, it struck him that this is one of his few clients who never asks, "What am I paying you?" Rather, this client measures the value of the relationship by the degree to which he feels cared for, and it has little to do with performance. He wants to know that his assets are where they are supposed to be, and that he feels safe and looked after.

So many of us focus on client retention strategies. We look at variables like the number of referrals we have received. We can overcomplicate ways to make our clients feel appreciated, from sporting events to fancy dinners, anything to retain solid footing in the relationship. Perhaps client retention is much simpler; perhaps it's a factor of caring more deeply, showing up in new ways; perhaps it's just about the way we are there.

Compete on Transparency

As your Baby Boomer clients enter their highest-earning years, many of them recognize that the paycheck at this level won't last forever. In some aspects of their life, spending is really dialed up—they may be buying second homes, taking trips, and expressing feelings of abundance with wine collections and art. Those same clients, though, are becoming more cost sensitive in other ways. Many of our clients understood this when either prospecting new business or reinforcing their value with existing clients. They're putting the portfolio and the cost of owning the funds at center stage. With prospective clients, they will present the cost of holding the funds, securities, and electronically traded funds or ETFs that the client currently holds and show it compared to the asset composite they would recommend. For existing clients, they will perform a similar exercise to reinforce the successful results being achieved for a fairly low cost.

This kind of transparency is mind-boggling and new to many clients. Most investors understand that they will pay a fee for the advice and guidance an advisor provides—and like all things that we value, most do not question the price of peace of mind.

But when presented with the choice of the same outcome for more or less fees, most would choose to pay less. Yet many portfolios are laddered with the unnecessary high fees that are often incurred just for holding certain securities or asset classes, in particular, hedge funds, private equity, or variable annuities, without the need or additional return to justify it.

Many times, though, these costs are buried, so clients may not even understand or, like the case of one of our advisors' prospective clients, an 80-year-old woman who was sold an expensive and illiquid variable annuity. When the proposal pointed this out, the shock and disappointment alone were enough reason to stop doing business with a product salesperson and seek to work with a fiduciary advisor.

Leading with transparency is also an appealing strategy for the Millennial generation, who we will cover soon. In fact, as we still seek to rebuild trust in our industry, transparency and authenticity are generation-agnostic strategies.

Be Brave and Have Hard Conversations

When we ask our clients what keeps them up at night, sometimes we hear the most unpredictable answers, like this one from a client "helping my client avoid making poor decisions."

Baby Boomers—Early and Trailing—often have significant wealth and can carry guilt or desire to help their children during tough or good times. Many Boomers watch their children go through divorces, buy homes, or want to fund an entrepreneurial spirit. They make substantial monetary gifts to fund these endeavors or bail their children out.

Yet this same advisor shared with us that he watched two clients go into debt because of their parental instinct to put love and help their children over their own financial needs and reason. One of the clients referred to in these scenarios watched their net worth drop from $5,000,000 to $500,000 because of their children's mismanagement of an opportunity. It is really hard to say no to our children, but when we make decisions only from the heart, the results can be devastating in retirement.

The best advisors help their clients understand the implications of their decisions. They work with them to forecast best- and worst-case scenarios, making sure the outcome is positive no matter which one should occur. They also help facilitate these discussions and provide their clients with ways or strategies to say no to a request while preserving the relationship. They are not afraid to intervene on their client's behalf or engage family counselors and family governance experts to help. In fact, we see family governance support as an important skill advisory firms are either staffing for or developing their own muscle around.

Talk about the Joneses

Our clients tell us that another poor choice their Boomer clients make is trying to keep up with the Joneses. Come mid-50s to early 60s, with some money in the bank and their careers on solid footing, many Baby Boomer clients start to look around and take stock of what their peer group and colleagues are up to. Our advisor clients tell us this is fatal for their Boomer clients. Some, from a financial perspective, stretch for things like second homes. Others can afford the financial component but have not thought through the emotional aspect of making choices because someone else made a similar one, versus their own authentic desires.

It's hard to help our clients escape the stream of messages from advertisers and the influence of people around them. Even wealthy people get in over their heads. Sixty percent of NBA and 78 percent of NFL players file for bankruptcy within five years of retirement.[13]

It is also difficult to help unwind younger Baby Boomer clients from comparisons in market performance, too. This competitive generation looks for places to compete everywhere, including how they are doing compared to the market averages. It takes some effort to retrain your clients to think only of the benchmarks they are trying to beat. It's similar to the older Boomers and Matures for whom fear can drive a singular focus on capital preservation without proper risk management. Those clients focused on performance are also driven by emotion and not prudence and reason. We have to help shift their thinking from beating someone or something (a benchmark) to thinking about the outcome they want for their life.

By now we know that a financial advisor's job is not one dimensional. It's not only about managing the money. We are also sounding boards and educators. Financial literacy programs are sorely lacking in our country, and providing insights around spending and saving often falls to the advisors. Advisors can also help with the emotional aspects of money.

Take Ross Levin, founder and president of Accredited Investors Wealth Management Inc. Ross has built his business around four tenets:

1. Wealth management
2. Professional advice
3. Money and values
4. Investment approach

This is a wheel, or a 360-degree view of his client's life. In the many conversations we have had with Ross, he never addresses only one plane, for example, the investments. Whether it is a plan to budget better or save for retirement, Ross seeks to first understand someone's values and their intention behind the money. He is not afraid to constructively challenge his clients, taking them through a Socratic process to separate wants and needs, the merits of giving your children everything from a financial perspective and the burdens of it too, or the joy of giving freedom. He has helped clients understand when they're really hungry for companionship or affection, for instance, and helps them identify resources and strategies to name those feelings rather than continue to indulge them, hoping the next new thing will bring relief.

---

[13] Holly Johnson, "The High Cost of Keeping Up With the Joneses," *Get Rich Slowly*, April 25, 2016. Available at: www.getrichslowly.org/blog/2014/06/18/the-high-cost-of-keeping-up-with-the-joneses/.

Ross is generous with his insights, not only with his clients, but in his weekly column, *Spend Your Life Wisely.* To become someone's trusted advisor, you need some basic skills. You have to be able to see the big picture and communicate well. But you also need to know how to have the hard conversations. You need to know how to tell the truth from an authentic and caring place. Ross is exceptional at this and it is the glue in his client generations from Baby Boomers on down.

Help Your Clients Protect What Matters

The average age for a man to experience a first heart attack is between 45 and 66.[14] It doesn't take your clients too many of these examples to start feeling some anxiety themselves and want to very quickly get their financial house in order. Baby Boomer clients will be more focused than most on working through the details of their estate plans, medical proxies, and living wills, and revisiting insurance policies. Most advisors understand this and have built out considerable networks and resources for clients to tap to ensure these foundational plans are in place.

It is a mistake to simply hand off these relationships to other professionals with expertise. The top-performing advisors remain connected and quarterback these relationships. They also use their trusted advisor skills and offer support to their clients as they think through the challenges of estate planning today, including:

- The implication of longer life spans
- More divorces and blended families
- Retirement accounts that have been severely affected by the financial crisis
- The need for long-term care and the reality that children of today's generation are much less likely to become caregivers of their parents
- Uncertainty of Social Security and defined benefit programs

The best advisory businesses see these networks as complementary and as partnerships, not competition. Advisors are a valuable partner to estate planners and can help craft a plan in a much more thorough way with their knowledge of the client relationship and their goals. The advisor's clients appreciate their continued involvement and tend to feel more at ease with the advisor present and looking over the documents and the decisions. When the

---

[14] Dennis Thompson Jr., "How Men Can Avoid Heart Attacks," *Everyday Health*, December 7, 2012. Available at: www.everydayhealth.com/mens-health/avoiding-heart-attacks.aspx.

advisor stays involved, clients tend to report a stronger sense of satisfaction with the relationship, as there's a sense that the advisor is connecting and overseeing all the providers: estate planners, insurance agents, accountants, and elder care specialists. It's an easy way to stay involved and demonstrate high marks on caring and accountability for the client's life.

CHAPTER 6

The Generation X Client

Reality Bites and Gen X Bites Back

Generation X at a Glance*:
- Born between 1965 and 1980
- Share of adult population: 27%
- Share of non-Hispanic white population: 61%
- Political affiliation: 32% Democrat; 21% Republican; 39% Independent
- Character traits: anti-establishment, self-reliant, individualistic, skeptical[†]

Top concerns for advisors to address:
- **Show them that two heads are better than one.** Gen X is the latchkey, do-it-yourself generation. They're used to going it alone, but that strategy has not always generated the best results. If your ego stays in check while they google, stalk, and challenge you, you can win this client over and offer them much-needed advice and insights to meet their goals.
- **Be authentic and transparent.** Trust has not fully recovered for the majority of the investing population and it's questionable if it was ever really there for Gen X. Gen X isn't easily fooled and anything that feels like a sales pitch is a turn-off. Show these clients what you can do for them. Case studies of peers facing similar challenges will work well to showcase your expertise and solutions. Don't forget to give them lots of detail, be up front about fees and potential downsides, and remain patient while they do their own research and make their decisions.

---

* Pew Research Center, "Millennials in Adulthood: Generations Defined," March 5, 2014. Available at: www.pewsocialtrends.org/2014/03/07/millennials-in-adulthood/sdt-next-america-03-07-2014-0-06/.

[†] Value Options, "Meet the Multigenerational Workforce," Beacon Health Options, September 5, 2012. Available at: www.valueoptions.com/spotlight_YIW/workforce.htm.

Generation Smarts: Working with Gen X Clients

John Cusack. Kurt Cobain. Singles. The O. J. Simpson trial. This antiestablishment generation of skeptics is 45 million Americans strong.[1] Generation X are individuals born between 1965 and 1980,[2] meaning in 2015 the first members of this generation turned 50.

They are the original grunge, flannel shirt-wearing latchkey kids. They remember the days before the Internet. They are the last generation of our society who is not born a technology native.

They are also deeply misunderstood and often forgotten, being both a much smaller and much shorter generation (only ~15 years) than the Boomers and Millennials they are squeezed between. Generation X is referred to as and often feels like society's neglected middle child,[3] and as a result they are a quieter and often overlooked generation.

Gen X's introverted nature is one part driven by their pessimistic view of the world and by the lack of a mirror from society. There is very little attention from media or business in trying to figure out these individuals, or at least compared to the obsession we have with the generations who bookend it.

Baby Boomers were hippies out to change the world. The Millennials after them have managed to make nearly every company and workplace, trying to reach them as consumer or employee, bend over backward for them (quite reminiscent of their helicopter parents).

However, like the X variable they are named for, this generation is unknown. Try to get through a day without reading a news headline or a work-related conversation about Boomers or Millennials, and you'll find it is tough! Now try the same exercise, listening in the media or our workplaces for cues about Gen X. Where Millennials and Boomers are seen as heavily contributing to the outcome of any situation: a presidential election (*"Millennials feel the Bern"*), the retirement crisis (*"Crisis building as Boomers begin retiring"*), and so on, it is hard to find evidence that Generation X is viewed as contributing the same impact in ways our society, political climates, consumer behaviors, and workplaces evolve.

---

[1] Cam Marston, "5 Ways to Win Over Gen X Investors," CNBC.com, July 17, 2014. Available at: www.cnbc.com/2014/07/17/5-ways-to-win-over-gen-x-investors.html.

[2] Pew Research Center, "The Whys and Hows of Generations Research," September 3, 2015. Available at: www.people-press.org/2015/09/03/the-whys-and-hows-of-generations-research/.

[3] Paul Taylor and George Gao, "Generation X: America's Neglected 'Middle Child,'" June 5, 2014. Available at: www.pewresearch.org/fact-tank/2014/06/05/generation-x-americas-neglected-middle-child/.

As much as they are often overlooked or unknown to companies, marketers, and demographers, they are also a little unknown to themselves. Receiving little feedback from the world coupled with a society that tends to be dismissive of them, Generation X lacks a mirror beyond the negative stereotypes and has struggled to define themselves, get a sense of their needs, or to learn how to ask for help.

Previous generations and those who come after Gen X tend to be steeped in optimism. From scandals, inflation, world crisis, and recessions, Gen X's formative years left them with plenty of reasons to justify the pessimism that many feel they were just born with.[4]

Labeled slackers and loners, this generation defied society's low expectations of them and succeeded in becoming responsible citizens who today solidly contribute to their professional and family lives.

This generation didn't look for trophies and validation. Rather than wait for someone to show them the way, they chose to go it alone in the sense of creating an edgy attitude and tough persona. When the topic comes to their finances, however, their propensity to go it alone, skepticism, and hesitancy to trust are hurting them in a big way.

You can always find proof to support what you want to believe and this is true for Generation X. This generation pushed through the church scandals and the divorces happening all around them in their childhood and adolescence. As life went on, things were looking up and their perseverance was rewarded.

In the early 2000s, as this generation was entering its 30s, they felt more enthusiastic about life and things around them seemed to be going well. The stock market hit new highs and buoyed their psyches with the promise of new and innovative technology companies. In their personal lives, Gen X was settling down, building families and professions. Many of them started to see their earning power and dreams materialize when the Great Recession hit.

This generation took it particularly hard, feeling not only the pain to their savings account, but the sting and old feelings that if there was one thing they could count on it was that things fall apart. It was the proof they needed to validate their cynicism and their belief that what feels too good to be true usually is.

Generation X was familiar with scandals and crises, but this time it was different. Growing up, bad news was mostly the headlines and a sign of the times that informed their psyche. This time it was personal. The Great Recession hit their savings and sense of well-being. From bailouts to the decimated

---

[4] Cam Marston, *The Gen-Savvy Advisor: Advising the Generations in the New Age of Uncertainty* (Mobile, AL: Generational Insights, 2015).

401(k) and savings accounts, Gen X used the crisis to refuel its pessimism and antiestablishment ways, and here is some of their evidence:

- Many Gen Xers bought homes just before the real estate crash. A recent Zillow study points to Gen X being more underwater in their homes than other generations.[5]
- Having bad timing in the housing market and the subsequent drop in prices was compounded by the stock market losses they faced and other lingering debts like student loans.
- Cam Marston's research shows that between 2007 and 2010, Generation X lost 45 percent of their wealth and their median net worth dropped from $75,000 to $42,000.[6] While these balances may seem insignificant to financial advisors who have minimums of $1M or more as a starting point, it's easy to extrapolate the effect on larger portfolios and on Gen X's fragile psyche.
- Richard J. Hagen's firm TradeKing conducted a study in September 2014 that showed investors aged 18 to 44 are the least likely to speak with an investment advisor—66 percent of the respondents were Gen X investors. His study also showed the top three reasons holding these potential clients back were cost, trust, and fear of judgment over their financial position and limited knowledge of finances. Richard reframes the last point as an interesting rhetorical statement: "I feel guilty I don't have a better handle on this critical area of my life!"[7]
- A study by TransAmerica says only 12 percent of the Gen X investors they surveyed feel that they have fully recovered from the Great Recession.[8]

The Great Recession caused many of these investors to retreat and it happened at the worst possible time. A study by Greenwald and Associates[9]

---

[5] Tim Logan, "Gen-X Remains Deepest Underwater on Home Mortgages," *Los Angeles Times*, August 26, 2014. Available at: www.latimes.com/business/realestate/la-fi-nearly-half-of-genxers-still-underwater-20140825-story.html.

[6] Cam Marston, "Gen X Investors Need Advisor Help," CNBC.com, September 9, 2014. Available at: www.cnbc.com/2014/09/08/gen-x-investors-need-advisor-help.html.

[7] Richard J. Hagen, Jr., "How Millennials and Generation X Can Conquer Their Fear of Finances," MarketWatch.com, December 12, 2014. Available at: www.marketwatch .com/story/how-millennials-and-generation-x-investors-can-conquer-their-fear-of-finances-2014-12-12.

[8] Transamerica Center for Retirement Studies, "Generation X Workers: 15 Alarming Facts about Retirement Readiness and 7 Steps for Improving It," August 2014. Available at: https://www.transamericacenter.org/docs/default-source/resources/center-research/tcrs2014_factsheet_generation_x.pdf.

[9] Globe Newswire, "New Study Reveals Generations X and Y Feel Behind on Retirement Savings," September 8, 2014. Available at: http://globenewswire.com/news-release/2014/09/08/664307/10097488/en/New-Study-Reveals-Generations-X-and-Y-Feel-Behind-on-Retirement-Savings.html.

found that the majority of Generation X has not calculated what they need to save for retirement.

It would be easy to, but we should not paint this generation's lack of planning with the same brush of laziness or apathy they tend to get painted with. The lack of a plan seems to be much more a product of fear and not knowing how to get started than not caring.

The Greenwald study shows that this generation believes saving for retirement is difficult, with 65 percent stating that they believe it's harder for their generation to save than it was for earlier generations; 48 percent feel like they are behind on their savings plans and only 43 percent feel satisfied with their current financial situation.

Each finding points to an opportunity for financial advisors to tap into these needs and guide this generation to better outcomes. It's also a call for advisors to put aside their bias that this generation is apathetic, difficult to work with, or not valuable as a client.

While often overshadowed and overlooked, Generation X investors deserve the attention of advisory firms and our industry. They are actively thinking about retirement, saving, and investing, and they want to engage. They are in their prime earning years and they need your help to take the first steps or validate and help them to cement their plans.

They also make good and loyal clients once you can get through to them and gain their trust. Amy Lynch's work concludes that Gen Xers "put their faith, not in groups, but in individuals." She notes that Gen Xers will be your toughest prospects, viewing any solution skeptically, asking the toughest questions, and welcoming or provoking conflict rather than easy consensus.[10] But once you have passed their muster, this Generation, like Lynch observes, will tend to put their faith in you. This is an excellent foundation for a long and loyal client relationship.

Despite all their skepticism and often gloomy outlook on the world, despite the ways they're overlooked, paying closer attention to Generation X is a smart idea for advisory businesses to pay attention to and build a critical bench of clients as both the heirs of Matures and Boomers and wealth creators in their own right.

Here are some reasons to believe:

- **It's their time:** Generation X is in leadership positions or on deck for senior positions in their firm and careers. They are earning and consuming more, buying homes, raising families, and getting serious about their

---

[10] Amy Lynch, "Decide Already! Gens Make Decisions Differently," Generational Edge, July 9, 2014. Available at: www.generationaledge.com/blog/decide-already-gens-make-decisions-differently.

finances. They are also the generation before the Millennials and poised to be significant inheritors of parent and grandparent wealth.

- **They need help and guidance.** Whether it is investing their own earnings or inherited funds, this generation needs strategies to plan for a sound retirement and the financial security that they crave. They need help with investing strategies and also, because they are in these peak years of balancing so many priorities, they also need strategies for college savings, managing the care of their children and parents, and estate planning—particularly insurance. This generation will also need your help navigating savings gaps, whether it is the burn of the recession, their propensity to be slow to save, or their general hesitancy.

- **They are good clients.** Generation X will make you work for their business and their trust. They can be incredibly frustrating as they research and kick the tires of your business. This generation is the ultimate slow yes. Generation X will thoroughly investigate any product or service they are considering, and what makes interaction with them so frustrating is how they push aside your help and desire to shepherd their evaluation process. This generation is not interested in the value proposition you spent hours crafting, PowerPoint slides, or sales pitches. They prefer to go about making big decisions as they've managed most things in their life—alone. They are online sleuths and will google you, seeking both online and off-line peer reviews. Generation X is the juxtaposition of a generation that seeks companies and people to be honest with them while simultaneously thinking that few will. The financial services industry, with its low trustworthy scores in general, has a lot of wood to chop to win over this generation. If you can get past their guarded demeanor with lots of straight talk and giving them space to make their assessments and come to their conclusions, it's our experience that Gen X clients become clients for life. They are loyal, they trust their process and decisions, and they are unlikely to challenge you as much as they are to relax in the confidence of their decisions.

Help Them to Visualize Success

It's hard to plan and achieve your goals without having a clear picture of success. This generation is adept at visualizing what can go wrong. In fact, that's their starting point and it's why Gen X needs your help to visualize what can go right. Your Gen X clients at first will doubt your optimism. One way to help keep them on track is to talk with them in a manner that is straightforward and simple. Pause a lot, make room for their questions and doubts. Listen to their concerns and be careful not to seem dismissive of them. Many advisors miss this with Gen X and take their doubts as a challenge to their expertise. If you can hold some space for their skepticism and really accept that it is part of their psyche and not personal, you will secure your relationship with your Gen X clients.

Similarly, when you present a plan and speak about the future, do it in a straightforward way. You will be viewed as really understanding this client if you produce a plan for the future along with transparency about what might go wrong, where, and when. When you're trying to present yourself as a guide to helping your clients achieve their goals, it may seem counterintuitive to be this forthcoming about risk. While it may seem that presenting a sunny view of the future would appeal to current and future clients, trust is built, especially with this generation, when we are real and humble, especially for Gen X. It will do a lot to build their trust. Being forthcoming and putting the worst-case scenarios out there can give you the perfect opportunity to subtly showcase your expertise as you also present strategies to manage these risks.

This do-it-yourself generation has come far on their own to figure life out, but they find themselves stuck when it comes to their finances. Helping them see what is possible while speaking to their desire for security and how it affects their investing decisions is a powerful way to connect with your Gen X clients.

Begin with the End in Mind

Gen Xers came to our workplaces along with the introduction of 401(k) plans and the decline in pensions and defined benefit plans. A recent Transamerica study noted this moment and called Gen X "the 401(k) generation."[11] Recognizing that they were on their own once again, Gen X took advantage of the new workplace savings plans available to them and began saving for retirement earlier than previous generations. In addition to recognizing that their companies and government could not be counted on to provide critical retirement benefits, innovation, and features like automatic enrollment, employer matches, and the inescapable break room poster calculating the future value of trading a Starbucks coffee for an extra $25 per week in savings all contributed to Gen X's willingness to save. Generation X's early start and the good habits that were encouraged, automatic payroll deductions notwithstanding, this generation is woefully underprepared for a solid retirement. Gen X simply hasn't saved enough and the recent market downturns have only exacerbated the situation.

There are a number of alarming trends (Table 6.1) that advisors need to bear in mind when working with these clients and also some amazing opportunities.

---

[11] See Note 9.

TABLE 6.1

Fact	Something to think about!
According to Employee Benefit News, 64 percent of Generation Xers have some money saved for retirement, but only 8 percent have saved enough. (http://www.benefitnews.com/news/generation-x-falling-short-on-retirement-preparedness)	Most Gen Xers have committed to their chosen life path by now. Whether that is pursuing a traditional career, starting a business, starting a family, or not. This is also a time when they may face some life challenges that can create significant financial setbacks: taking time off to raise children, divorce, and beginning to care for elderly parents. Most Gen Xers know they need to be saving more and many do not know where to begin.
	Help your Gen X clients understand their "number" and create a feasible and desirable path to achieving it. Be sure to help them consider both sides of their balance sheet—assets and debts—and face the truth about where they stand, no matter how difficult. Facing the facts about our financial situations can conjure up the dread similar to stepping on the scale or opening a monthly credit card statement. We may not like the number, but without knowing where we stand, we have little hope of making the necessary changes or plans that move us along to our desired state. Gen X is counting on you to help them get a true picture of reality and a plan for success. Caught between the squeeze of mounting responsibilities and running out of time to save, they need your help and are urgently looking for advisors with solutions and the patience to guide them.
Northwestern mutual finds that 34 percent of Generation X does not know how much they will need to retire. (https://www.northwesternmutual.com/about-us/studies/planning-and-progress-2015-study)	If we had health issues we wouldn't guess at the diagnosis, yet when it comes to our finances, there's a tendency to rely on bias and guesswork. Our brains are very good at synthesizing information and piecing together stories. We can process a lot of variables and we often guess right—this is the foundation of overconfidence. Generation X does not have the time or extra savings to accommodate a margin of error. They cannot fund their dreams on estimates.
	Once your clients have transparency, clarity, and a view of how they are doing, it's time to help them analyze their cash flow and start working on building a better budget. Many Gen Xers understand their basic savings and investing options. Gen X knows it needs to save more. What's missing is access to education and solutions that can help make saving easier. You will stand out if you can provide this kind of unique education to help your clients understand their options as well as any possibilities to fast-track their savings and investment plans.

Fact	Something to think about!
	For example, can you encourage your clients to take full advantage of their employer-sponsored 401(k) or 403(b) program, including catch-up provisions? Can you help them develop good habits like maximizing deferrals, avoiding loans, and early withdrawals? Remember, Gen X has their own bias to not trust or value a financial advisor. If you can help them remove the guesswork and be straightforward, you will build solid relationships with these slow-to-trust, difficult-to-please clients. You'll be more successful relating to this client if you chunk your advice into small, manageable goals. Help your clients zoom in and zoom out on achieving their short-term goals, work through immediate obstacles, and keep an eye on the big picture. If you can do this, you will endear this valuable Gen X client to you and your business in deep ways.
Northwestern Mutual's "Planning and Progress Study" found that 66 percent of Gen Xers think they need to improve their financial planning skills; 23 percent are "not at all confident" that they can reach their financial goals. (https://www.northwesternmutual.com/about-us/studies/planning-and-progress-2015-study)	This generation has so much going on managing their family life and professional lives, even when they agree with your recommendations, they may have a hard time following through. The financial advisors we admire use the natural human tendency to procrastinate, or get distracted, as an opportunity for regular and consistent communications.

Ross Levin's firm, for example, sends a list of agreements after each meeting. His relationship team sets to work scheduling check-ins, helping their clients tick off each goal or to-do as it's achieved. For Ross's firm, it's an incredible tool to stay close to their client. For a Gen X client, it's a tremendous way to add value and help them feel a greater sense of accomplishment with their lives. |
| The Transamerica Center for Retirement Studies finds that 65 percent would like more education and advice from their employers on how to reach their retirement goals. | With so many Gen Xers craving education and help planning for their retirement, one way to scale your service model to meet this need is to take advantage of Gen X's propensity and preferences for "do-it-yourself" business models. You can offer access to learning through electronic channels, pointing these clients to blog posts, articles, and links to educational websites. There are many nonprofit financial literacy sites that make their content available for sharing that are good sources for content. See, for example, the Institute for Financial Literacy: https://financiallit.org.

Firms and advisors who are more sophisticated and embrace technology in their businesses may want to consider adding a marketing automation system to their customer relationship management (CRM) platforms. These systems can help advisors increase the quality and effectiveness of their customer experience overall. Think of it as an extension of your service model, strengthening high-tech interactions with digital touch points that can feel just as personal. |

(Continued)

TABLE 6.1 (*Continued*)

Fact	Something to think about!
	We see the top firms creating personalized campaigns. These campaigns may be segmented client, topic, or other criteria. What many firms appreciate about marketing automation is the ability to schedule ahead marketing activities that are proactive, not reactive. You can think of this as a marketing tool that can provide "air cover" to support your existing business development needs. While you may schedule in-person or high-tech client meetings on average once per quarter, marketing automation allows you to schedule e-mails, web posts, and other communications ahead of time, allowing you to stay front and center with your prospects or clients and keeping a dialogue going.
	You can drip the educational materials and information your clients crave before they have to ask for it—or even know that they need it. You can create campaigns around life events and automatically schedule educational material deliveries. You can craft "personas" and campaigns that align with the needs and desires of that niche. One example could be Gen Xers turning 50 and needing to accelerate their savings. For this group, you can schedule a campaign in advance of their fiftieth birthday to help them understand their options and eligibility for catch-up contributions in their 401(k), 403(b), and 457 plans, and IRAs, as appropriate.
	Today's digital world is full of short attention spans and competing messages. One of the most powerful ways to ensure your communications are opened, appreciated, and your clients and prospects are taking the actions you want them to take is to send communications that build trust. Your role as advisor implies it is a trusted one. But for your client to build trust that you understand them and that your e-mails are worth their time to read and interact with requires some work on your part. The best programs aim for consistency in timing, and delivering high quality content that is insightful and engaging. This is what makes educational content so powerful. In terms of content, it is about their other interests. When it's well timed and thoughtfully executed, the ways marketing automation and campaigns can help deliver, it builds a pattern of trust, showing your clients that you understand them, are anticipating their needs, and are giving them the security and feel-good predictability that you are thinking of them and their well-being. Offer solutions proactively; don't wait for them to raise an issue or concern.
	As efficient as e-communications are, they are no substitute for taking the time to connect with these clients in person and maintain your high-tech interactions.

Fact	Something to think about!
	The personas you develop for your e-mail campaigns can inform your in-person interactions, too. A top firm in New York, with whom we've worked extensively, focuses their practice on the needs of high-net-worth divorced female clients. Many of these women have not been as closely involved with their finances as their ex-husbands or partners. In order to build their confidence managing money and budgeting, these newly divorced clients are required to visit the office each month to receive their statement. At this time, the relationship manager tasked with overseeing the relationship walks the client through the statement review. Along the way, they are pointing out the asset classes, account balances, areas to pay closer attention to, and the risks to manage. This once-a-month meeting solidifies the relationship and provides these clients with a much-needed and much-appreciated boost to their financial literacy and confidence. A combination of approaches is a solid path to consider. Whatever you provide, be sure it's simple, easy to understand, and you're checking in regularly with your clients to see if it's meeting their needs, the right level of support, and contains appropriate and actionable ideas for follow-up.
	Many advisory firms struggle to understand, never mind calculate, a return on investment on their marketing and business development activities. When you invest in marketing automation and tie the campaigns to your CRM, you will receive, over time, powerful information on what messages resonate with your clients. You will be able to see what content assets, campaigns, or conversations activated a new prospect relationship or further cultivated an existing client relationship.
	For those firms with a chief marketing officer or dedicated management focused on business development, investing in data-driven tools like marketing automation can help your firm move from measuring soft metrics like brand awareness and vanity metrics like web clicks, hits, and search results to better measure significant impacts to your revenue, profits, and pipeline development. This will yield better results for your business, as you'll soon be able to accelerate programs that are working and discontinue those that no longer work; but you'll also help your marketing and business development teams establish professional credibility and a seat at the leadership table. Too many advisory firm owners are still too dependent on their individual rainmaking abilities or find that they are afraid of investing in efforts that feel reminiscent of a time in their career when what they sold was more important than the relationships they developed. We need to help reshape those perceptions. We need to give owners of advisory businesses the same tools to anticipate client needs, spark client conversations, and proactively address the unspoken needs and questions weighing on our clients' minds that big firms with big marketing teams and budgets have.

(Continued)

TABLE 6.1 (*Continued*)

Fact	Something to think about!

	Investing in marketing as a science is a powerful tool to level the playing field. Some market-ready solutions advisory firms may want to consider include:
	
	• *Act-on* (https://www.act-on.com/)
	• *Marketo* (https://www.marketo.com/)
	• *Oracle*: https://www.oracle.com/marketingcloud/products/marketing-automation.html
	• And for those firms that need help with content and campaign development, consider:
	   • *Vestorly* (https://www.vestorly.com/) and
	   • *Heresay Social*: (http://hearsaysocial.com/)

The Insured Retirement Institute finds that 77 percent of Gen X workers do not use a financial planner when saving for retirement. Those that do have saved nearly twice as much as those who go it alone. (https://www.myiri-online.org/docs/default-source/research/the-retirement-readiness-of-generation-x-january-2014.pdf?sfvrsn=2)	We've talked about the rich potential of Generation X as clients, so this statistic should really underscore the opportunity. Today's financial advisor's clients in some ways can be considered a diminishing asset. Mature and Baby Boomer clients will soon be in the drawdown phase of their assets. No longer creating wealth and aging, the attributes of these clients from a long-term business perspective need to be examined. It's clear that advisors need to look to the next generation and it's clear that there's an oversupply of clients in need of professional financial guidance. So why are these clients without advisors? The issue seems to be twofold, with bias, hesitation, and uncertainty for how to engage existing with both advisors and investors. Advisors have a long history and strong bonds with many of their older clients. They have often worked together so long that these relationships are often pleasurable—friendships, really—and advisors may naturally (often unknowingly) turn more of their attention to these more-established relationships even if they do not need the nurturing and development that newer and fledging relationships require or would benefit from. Advisors also have their share of bias. They may have wrongly concluded that Generation X and its younger generation brethren are too far from retirement or do not have enough assets to require or value their services. Many advisors are dispelling this and finding that although their clients have a long runway until retirement, they are still hungry for advice, information, and a relationship with someone who can provide them with steady counsel.

Fact	Something to think about!
	On the other hand, investors themselves contribute to the low match rate between advisor and investor. There is considerable reluctance from younger investors to seek out and invest in a relationship with a financial advisor. For starters, many Gen Xers and their younger siblings, the Millennials, tend to be conservative investors. Many feel permanently scarred by the Great Recession. These investors project their own bias and may wrongly associate financial advisors with managing more risky investment options like stocks rather than helping find more stable and consistent assets like cash management strategies and real estate.* Many of these potential clients do not seek an advisor because of a lack of confidence. Having few experiences of being proactively sought out by advisors and hearing a regular refrain of being "too small," many clients are fearful of not feeling valued or of being rejected. Instead, these potential clients find themselves consulting friends, family, investing peer groups, or even the Internet and social media for investment advice. Others would simply prefer to do it themselves. On account of trust issues, a feeling their advisors don't understand them, or simply falling back on their infamous "do-it-yourself" attitude, many affluent Gen Xers who do not have a financial advisor say that they prefer and are deeply engaged in managing their own wealth. These do-it-yourself younger investors value someone to validate their decisions. There's an attraction for these investors to an advisor who is willing to collaborate, share the investing process with, allow these clients to be actively involved, and hear them out about certain investment preferences, for example, social finance and ways they can ensure their investing decisions contribute positively to their communities.

(Continued)

81

TABLE 6.1 (*Continued*)

Fact	Something to think about!
	The appeal of digital advice, more transparency, and lower costs may be other drivers of the reluctance to use a traditional financial advisor. While the business model is new, Gen Xers are considerably comfortable with technology, and a good look "under the hood" does not highlight too many differences in investing approaches. For example, most "robo" or digital advisors still rely on the same investing principles—modern portfolio theory, examining and adapting for risk tolerance, and time horizons and so on— and provide this generation with a comfort that the services they will receive at a fraction of the cost is worth a hard look. These digital business models are also appealing to these next-gen investors because they remove some of previously mentioned obstacles. There is little fear of rejection for being too small or insignificant when you're perusing a website or filling out an online application. The business model is also at the intersection of Gen X's desire for do-it-yourself (they can view balances, research investments, and interact socially with other like-minded investors) while still providing them with high-tech interactions and thoughtful guidance when needed or their investing situations become too complex. These digital solutions are also a tempting substitute for a real advisor because of the promise of their mobile and frictionless client experience. The financial services industry has largely escaped disruption. Some of the most exciting innovations in recent years come from these digital advice providers. These business models have good timing and are riding the wave of high customer demand for smooth client experiences, transparency, low cost, simplification, and ease of doing business. We believe real advisors and real relationships will always have an advantage. What makes these firms easy to dismiss by some is that they think there is no human interaction. This needs to be reconsidered and challenged. On the other side of the click, the e-mail, or interaction are often talented financial professionals and advisors as committed to solving their client's problems as those who operate in traditional business models. The good news is, the digital space is not limited to a few players. There are many white-label options available for advisory firms to consider so they can continue to offer their traditional services while experimenting with this model and engaging with the next-generation client effectively and in a way that's compelling to them.

*Suelain Moy, "Why Investors Prefer Real Estate Stocks, Bonds and Gold," July 22, 2015. Available at: www.thefiscaltimes .com/2015/07/22/Why-Investors-Prefer-Real-Estate-Stocks-Bond-and-Gold.

Source: Employee Benefit News (2016), Northwestern Mutual (2015), Transamerica Center for Retirement Studies (2014), and the Insured Retirement Institute (2014).

CHAPTER 7

Millennials

The Mass-Misunderstood

Millennials at a glance*:
- Born after 1980
- Share of adult population: 27%
- Share of non-Hispanic white population: 57%
- Political affiliation: 50% Independent; 27% Democrat; 17% Republican
- Character traits: overconfident, optimistic, digitally enabled, strong sense of entitlement

Top concerns for advisors to address:
- **Give them a plan.** Millennials have an arduous journey to a secure retirement. Working with you on a plan that steps them through it can help it feel more manageable to get started and stick with it.
- **Give them confidence.** Dubbed the Recession Generation, Millennials need your help to see this defining moment of their formative years with new eyes. You can help them find more balanced attitudes surrounding risk taking, savings, and equity investments, and give them solutions to ensure that they take appropriate risk taking and sound financial steps to achieve their goals.
- **Be relevant.** Design a service experience that resonates. Get turned on, not turned off, by the Millennial generation's impatience, desire for the latest technology, longing for appreciation and self-esteem builders, and social nature. Find ways to build these expectations into your service model.

*www.pewsocialtrends.org/2014/03/07/millennials-in-adulthood/sdt-next-america-03-07-2014-0-06/.

2015 was the year that the Millennial generation surpassed the Baby Boomer generation as the largest living generation in the United States.[1] By comparison, Generation X is not predicted to outnumber the Baby Boomer generation until 2028. The sheer size of this generation underscores the magnitude and impact Millennials will have not only as consumers but in our workplaces and our society.[2]

Born between 1980 and 2000, these Americans are estimated to number 75 million to 80 million. When immigration projections are factored in, the Millennial population is estimated to peak at 81.1 million by 2036. The Census Bureau projects that the Gen X population will peak at 20 million individuals fewer than this, reaching a mere 65.8 million in 2018.

Sheer size is only one factor generating the attention paid to this generation and why they may indeed be the most important generation our society has yet encountered.

- 2015 marked the year that Millennials became the largest generation in the workforce, with more than one in three workers identifying as Millennial.[3]
- Millennials are our country's most important customer segment, accounting for $1.3 trillion in direct annual spending, $430 billion of which is considered discretionary and nonessential spending. It also does not include the spending this generation's influences of their parents and grandparents.[4]
- Millennials are the most educated generation in our country's history to date. Sixty-one percent of adult millennials have attended college compared to 46 percent of the Baby Boomer generation.[5]
- Millennials are the most racially diverse generation. They are described as a transitional generation, with 43 percent of Millennial adults identifying as nonwhite, which is the highest percentage of any generation.[6]
- Millennials were born into an era exploding with new technology and new media, and as a result technology has always felt like a natural and necessary part of life, not something they need to adopt. Their childhood

---

[1] www.pewresearch.org/fact-tank/2015/01/16/this-year-millennials-will-overtake-baby-boomers/

[2] Ibid.

[3] Ibid.

[4] Ibid.

[5] https://www.whitehouse.gov/sites/default/files/docs/millennials_report.pdf.

[6] www.pewsocialtrends.org/2014/03/07/millennials-in-adulthood/.

experiences with technology labeled them Digital Natives and informed what they expect in nearly all instances—from making purchasing decisions to education and work—and companies have been trying to understand and adjust to their preferences ever since.

* Millennials understand their influence on brands, governments, and institutions. They're using their optimism and belief that they can change the world to do just that.

A generation of this size and influence becomes an easy one to stereotype. In our desire to understand how to adapt our businesses, build personas, qualify their needs, and learn how to structure our offerings to serve them, we deeply risk overgeneralizing. Like our work with women, and our proclamation that "women are not a niche," it is important to recognize that this rings true for all of our customer segments.

In our work with women, we showed that women are not a niche; they are 51 percent of the demographic. But, within the women's demographic are many important niches: women as wealth creators, widows, business owners, same-sex couples, and so on.

It's important to do the same for the Millennial generation. While we can make some broad generalizations based on the moments we described earlier that have informed their generational views and perceptions, we must be certain not to overgeneralize.

The Boston Consulting Group (BCG) identified six Millennial segments that are worth considering as you develop client and prospect personas and experiences for these clients in your own business. We've considered the BCG model and have added on some considerations of our own that may appeal or make your business offering more relevant to each segment.

Table 7.1 uses BCG's names for market segmentation groups and applies them to the advisory industry.

Generation Smarts: Working with Millennial Clients

Millennials are often accused of being overprotected, overpraised, and micromanaged by their parents and teachers. For most of their life, this generation lived in a bubble created in part by their Baby Boomer parents, and the sheer luck of being born and raised in good times. In fact, until the Great Recession of 2008, life was good, easy, programmed, and planned for these individuals.

The Great Recession was difficult for all generations, but the Millennial generation took it particularly hard. Millennials couldn't escape the crisis. It

TABLE 7.1

Segment	Traits	Advisor Strategy
Hip-ennial: "I can make the world a better place."	Cautious consumer, globally aware, charitable, and information hungry Greatest user of social media but does not push/contribute content Female dominated, below-average employment (many are students and homemakers)	Investing strategies like social finance may have an appeal to this client. Frame conversations around helping these investors properly protect and grow their wealth while pursuing social objectives that are meaningful to them.
Gadget Guru: "It's a great day to be me."	Successful, wired, free-spirited, confident, feels at ease Feels this is his best decade Greatest device ownership, pushes/contributes to content Male dominated, above average income, single	Consider bolting on a robo or online service model to your existing advisory services. High-tech delivery of personalized, data-driven, automated advice, and online tools at lower fees may appeal to this segment.
Millennial Mom: "I love to work out, travel, and pamper my baby."	Wealthy, family-oriented, works out, confident, and digitally savvy High online intensity Highly social and information hungry Can feel isolated from others by her daily routine Older, highest income	Be sure to engage her in the financial planning process. Reflect in her unique needs and responsibilities in her individual or family plan. This includes planning and protection for living longer, unexpected life events, education and opportunities to save for children's college, and ensuring any lingering student debt is addressed while she saves for her future and family's well-being.
Clean and Green Millennial: "I take care of myself and the world around me."	Impressionable, cause driven, healthy, green, and positive Greatest contributor of content, usually cause related Male dominated, youngest, more likely to be Hispanic, full-time student	Social finance may have an appeal to this consumer. Before they can invest in meaningful ways, help them sketch out a plan for paying down their debt, understanding their expenses, and planning for major purchases such as a wedding, car, or home. Build engagement with this client by teaching and offering tools to support budget management and share the peace of mind that comes with good financial habits.

86

Segment	Traits	Advisor Strategy
Anti-Millennial: "I'm too busy taking care of my family and my business and my family to worry about much else."	Locally minded, conservative Does not spend more for green products and services Seeks comfort and familiarity over excitement/change/interruption Slightly more female, more likely to be Hispanic and from the western United States	This client may resemble Gen X more than any Millennial stereotype. Aim to be more business-as-usual and respect their boundaries and desire for fewer distractions. While generational stereotypes suggest that this generation would embrace companies connecting with them over social media, a recent survey by BNY Mellon shows that the majority of Millennials prefer to reserve social media channels for interacting with friends and family.[7] Your effort may be more rewarded by speaking to their needs around preparing a budget, balancing career responsibilities with enjoying life, and building an emergency savings plan.
Old-School Millennial: "Connecting on Facebook is too impersonal. Let's meet up for coffee instead!"	Not wired, cautious consumer, and charitable Confident, independent, and self-directed Spends least amount of time online, reads Older, more likely to be Hispanic	If the Anti-Millennial more closely resembles Generation X, then the "Old-School Millennial" may relate to you more like their Boomer parents than others typical of their generation. Regardless of how they identify, most Millennials are heavily influenced by and have close relationships with their parents. Millennials tend to view their parents as their "go to" advisors and the people they trust for information and advice on most areas of their life, including financial matters. Designing strategies that connect Boomers and their children for educational sessions and client appreciation and engagement events is a smart idea.

7 https://www.bnymellon.com/_global-assets/pdf/our-thinking/generation-lost.pdf

Source: Market segments and traits come from Boston Consulting Group.

filled every news headline and every dinner conversation. They watched the tremendous and personal toll it took on their parents, neighbors, and communities' financial well-being.

Whereas previous generations had witnessed, lived through, and largely recovered from market ups and downs, for the Millennials, it was a first. They had very little context or ability to keep it in perspective. It was a shock for a generation who for most of its existence was largely protected, carefully looked after, and told they could do no wrong. This generation was regularly told that they were special, prized, and that things would always go well for them. They were taught to not settle, to hold out for the best—and they did. They had no reason to think otherwise until the bubble broke in such a profound way.

Don't Let Them Downsize Their Dreams

Beginning their careers at a time of record unemployment was the first financial setback of many for this generation. Although unemployment has fallen to 5.4 percent,[8] Millennials have yet to benefit or materially experience it, in terms of plentiful opportunity or meaningful wages. Forty-four percent of college graduates in their 20s feel stuck in "low-wage, dead-end jobs."[9] The number of Millennials who make less than $25,000 is at its highest level since the 1990s,[10] with almost a third of Millennials making less than $10,000 a year from their jobs.[11] Those Millennials who have found work cannot make ends meet alone, with 40 percent[12] of this generation stitching together a living combining their meager salaries with support from their families. Wealth inequality is already a hot topic in our country and its impact is significantly felt by the Millennial generation. We can see this clearly when we juxtapose the 28 million Millennials making less than $10,000 each year to the 720,000 of their peers in their generation's 1 percent making $106,500.[13]

While these statistics are sobering, we can't afford to let the Millennial generation wallow in bad news or downsize their dreams.

---

[8] www.forbes.com/sites/ashleystahl/2015/05/11/the-5-4-unemployment-rate-means-nothing-for-millennials/#78333f57d462.

[9] Ibid.

[10] Ibid.

[11] www.kansascity.com/news/business/personal-finance/article40955250.html.

[12] Ibid.

[13] Ibid.

This generation is forming its spending and savings habits now, and one of the best tools we have to help shape them into responsible investors and great clients is education.

One way to connect with the Millennials through education is to expand the ways we think about education. Here are some suggested topics and ways to get started:

- We have an obligation to help this Recession Generation understand that we have all experienced the best and worst of financial markets and how critical it is to see these as moments, not the final outcome. Help the Millennial generation see that time is on their side and the historical stock market trends show great returns over time. Share your wisdom to help reshape their perceptions, give them perspective, and build their financial literacy muscle.
- Many Millennial investors or children of your Boomer clients feel they have too little savings, or to be more frank: no money to invest. Where there is high unemployment, there is usually low savings and investing. Still, there will be a day when these potential clients' situation dramatically changes or they experience an inheritance windfall. Spend the time now teaching them how to build and manage a budget. Planning a drip e-mail campaign or, even better, a study group for the children of your Boomer clients to learn about these topics is a powerful engagement strategy. Help them build good habits. Some topics you can potentially explore include:
  - Building an emergency savings plan.
  - Debt management and reduction strategies.
  - Maximizing their contributions in 401(k) and IRA accounts, starting a 529, and the benefits of automating contributions.
  - Understanding their attitudes about money, impulse buying, and discretionary spending patterns.
  - Don't let them continue to feel uneasy about stocks. If it makes sense for their goals and objectives, help them ease into this asset class by researching and exploring socially responsible companies.

Communicate with Integrity and Clearly to Build Trust

For the advisors we work with, one of the most difficult consequences of the financial crisis is the bad press that surrounds them. Headlines swarm about the lack of investors' trust and if it will ever recover. Having the actions of a few bad apples tarnish the efforts of so many trustworthy professionals is one of the most personal and difficult consequences of the crisis to accept. That said, things are what they are and acknowledging Millennials' distrust of the financial markets, their perception of high fees, and lack of transparency are just a few of the concerns we need to address if we want to sincerely engage these clients.

Some of the ways we've learned from both Cam Marston and our own client experiences that can help rebuild trust with this generation include:

- *Avoid jargon.* For all generations, avoiding jargon and speaking in a straight-forward way is a good idea. For Millennials, who are astute at sniffing out authenticity, it's critical.
- *Be authentic and transparent.* There's no need to be anything you're not with this cohort of clients. Trying to act young and hip will only diminish your credibility. Be yourself and direct, while keeping in mind their unmet needs and unanswered questions. This generation is comfortable being friends with their parents and parents' friends. The relationship you form with them will feel familiar and will be welcome if you relate to them in the ways that matter to them (rather than leaning on the attributes and successes that may drive your esteem and self-value).
- *Recognize the power of their peers.* Previous generations trusted institutions and people based on their hierarchy. This generation trusts people. The trusted people in their lives are much more likely to be their peer groups and networks than any expert. Millennials are more comfortable with, and tend to rely much more on, the experience of their peers than any expert—however deep their qualifications. Google yourself and your firm regularly, check out the reviews and strategically develop your online presence as well as other channels where your next-generation clients may look to learn more about you. Welcome reviews and create opportunities for your Millennials to connect with one another. Let these clients know that personally interacting with them and their feedback is important to you.
- *Communicate consistently.* One of the simplest and often most neglected ways to build trust is to simply be consistent. This is important in our behavior and interactions and also in our ability to regularly add value. One way to do this with Millennials is through your communication strategy. Think beyond traditional touch points. For example, if you send monthly statements to all of your clients, how can you sweeten this for your Millennial investors? Can you provide positive affirmations and reward them for reaching their goals? Create mile markers that show their progress against goals like paying off debt or achieving home ownership. These can be delivered through phone calls or electronic methods. Today's advisory firms

are integrating these value-added touch points into their client experience with the help of technology, for example, sending daily texts with feedback, breaking down the financial plan into simple to-do lists, making themselves available for video consultations and collaboration, and even the gamification of investing to help their clients learn more about investing strategies and build their comfort levels in low-risk environments.

Embrace the Paradox

Think tanks, media, and industry pundits all make big generalizations about the Millennial generation. There is a tendency to take a fact, like the tech-savvy nature of this generation, and extrapolate it too broadly. Here are some contradictions of the Millennial generation that we need to consider if we want to connect and relate to this client. Keep these points in mind:

• **Digital Natives with Social Media Skepticism.** While Millennials may prefer digital channels like SnapChat, texting, instant messaging platforms, or e-mail for the majority of their communications, our research found a paradox. BNY Mellon's paper "The Generation Game: Savings for the New Millennial"[14] found that while Millennials are generally comfortable interacting with consumer brands over social media, they are turned off when financial services companies use these channels to connect with them. The highest-ranked channels for interacting with a financial services firm, according to the study, are:
  ○ Website/e-mail (40 percent)
  ○ Face to face (23 percent)
  ○ Telephone (18 percent)

  Demand for social media interaction was almost nonexistent. The study indicates that Millennials prefer to reserve social media as a space to interact with peers and friends. Some had harsh words (like silly and creepy) for firms that attempt to connect with them in their social space. Before making a blanket assumption that all Millennial clients will want to engage with you or your brand in their social channels, be sure to take the extra step to check in, not only for permission but for guidelines on the type of content they would like to receive.

---

[14] https://www.bnymellon.com/_global-assets/pdf/our-thinking/business-insights/the-generation-game.pdf

- **Digital Natives Who Like a Personal Touch.** While it's easy to bucket all Millennials as wanting a digital advice delivery experience, we found another paradox here. While it's true that Millennials who are cost-sensitive or have less to invest may prefer a purely digital channel or robo experience, there does come a time when they value human interaction. Millennials are validators by nature and they regularly check in with parents and peers for guidance. The same is true for their financial advisor. In our experience, the desire for face-to-face validation generally happens when Millennial clients reach an asset level of ~$150,000, or find themselves responsible for outcomes beyond themselves (for example, they've been entrusted to care for their parents' financial or other well-being).
- **Their Parents Are Their Most Trusted Advisor.** Millennials were cared for and groomed by their parents. The parents of Millennial children sought balanced lives, investing as much in their children as in their careers. The hours they put into work they extended to their children. This created some loss of the usual parent-child hierarchy, and a friendship tended to develop between the two generations. As a result, their parents are their confidants and trusted advisors. The BNY Mellon study "The Generation Game: Savings for the New Millennial" found Millennials overwhelmingly identified their parents as their primary source of advice on financial planning matters.
  - 52 percent said they would turn to their parents first for financial advice
  - 24 percent a bank
  - 16 percent a financial advisor
  - 10 percent friends
  - 2 percent insurance agent

CHAPTER 8

Generation Z and Beyond

Generation Z at a Glance*,†

- Born between 1995 and 2010
- Estimated at 72 million people
- Demographic breakdown: 55% Caucasian; 24% Hispanic; 14% African-American, and 4% Asian
- Character traits: connected creators

---

*http://adage.com/article/cmo-strategy/move-millennials-gen-z/296577/.

†www.huffingtonpost.com/daniel-burrus/gen-z-will-change-your-wo_b_9150214.html.

While the Millennials still dominate our headlines and attention, we cannot let our definition of the "Next Gen" end there. Generation Z is our country's most powerful cohort developing right behind the Millennials, and the oldest turned 20 in 2016. Generation Z is 75 million strong and it is imperative that we pay attention to the people they are growing into.

If the Millennials were considered Digital Natives, Generation Z was literally born with a device in their hand. Their personal heroes are "YouTubers." Generation Z is the first generation for which video games are a spectator sport. Amazon's purchase of Twitch for $970 million validates this trend and preference. Most of us have a difficult time getting our heads around why watching other people play video games would have any appeal—never mind trying to understand the implications of a generation that does. But Twitch, founded in 2011, is now the fourth-largest source of U.S. Internet traffic, behind Netflix, Google, and Apple.[1]

The popularity of YouTubers, SnapChat, and Periscope can give us some insight into preferences of this generation. Previous generations experienced the world in a very limited way, mostly through carefully curated content from a limited number of news outlets. Gen Z is knocking down walls and borders and disrupting not only how and where the world will consume content, but what kind of content is valued. Their choice today is a highly unedited and very personal content that in many ways mirrors the connection with the borderless world they desire.

There are no limits for the connections Gen Z creates, and few barriers. A colleague of ours shared that his daughter's school assigned an online scavenger hunt. We remarked how previous generations would have pulled a team together with the local kids from school and the neighborhood. Compare this to his daughter, who, within three days, had built a virtual team that included students from schools in Asia, Europe, and South America to set out on her mission. Supporting this point, a recent study showed 50 percent of international 8- to 12-year-olds are online daily and 25 percent are engaging with peers in other countries every day.[2]

This generation is not only limitless in how it evaluates physical barriers. Generation Z also feels limitless in their sense of what's possible:

- Achieving influencer and celebrity status used to involve a significant amount of talent, hard work, and luck. For Gen Z, it's within the reach of anyone with a webcam. Where big brands struggle to develop content that creates followers, Gen Z influencers, or YouTubers, find it easy to connect with millions of followers from their basement.
- Redefining relationship. For Generation Z, virtual and augmented reality offers a tremendous ability to disrupt how this generation connects and engages. Coupled with social media, augmented reality will change everything for how individuals meet, interact, and build relationships. It will also change the ways brands connect with consumers. The promise of these technologies is to bring technology into our world. You won't read a newspaper or search for information; it will all come to you and be a part of our natural environments. It's too soon to tell what these products will be or what industries will come from them, but we suggest taking a look

---

[1] www.wsj.com/articles/amazon-to-buy-video-site-twitch-for-more-than-1-billion-1408988885.
[2] www.fuelyouth.com/blog/generation-z-and-the-new-principles-of-interaction-design/.

at the vision of companies like Magic Leap (www.magicleap.com) to get a sense of how differently learning, working, and interacting will be in the not-too-distant future.

Generation Z is just beginning to experience the moments that will inform the lenses they see the world through, but early indications point to this generation becoming one of the most independent thinking and creative we have ever seen. While it may seem contradictory, this generation is one of the most realistic, too (no surprise, considering their Gen X parents). Here are some points to keep in mind as you consider Gen Z.

- The Millennial generation may be the last one to be raised with the American Dream in mind. Unlike their Millennial cohort, Generation Z was not taught to unabashedly follow their bliss. Rather, Gen X, largely the parents of Generation Z, their own skepticism notwithstanding, has witnessed the Great Recession, more war, and global unsettledness. As a result, Gen Z has been raised to be and think practical.[3]
- Born pinching, zooming, and swiping, Generation Z's ease of technology, along with their creativity, is creating an unprecedented generation of want-to-be entrepreneurs. A recent study shows 72 percent of high school students want to start a business someday compared to 64 percent of college students. Sixty-one percent of high school students want to be an entrepreneur rather than an employee compared to 43 percent of college students. Children in grades 5 through 12 respond similarly with 42.1 percent stating plans to start their own business. Almost 50 percent of the schools surveyed now offer classes in how to start and run a business, and almost 40 percent believe they will invent something that changes the world.[4]
- Generation Z's creativity is buoyed by the technology revolution around them. There is no adopting of technology—it's a ubiquitous part of their lives. Cultural influencers on YouTube and SnapChat inspire them to try their hand at creating original content, use 3D printers at home to bring their ideas to life, and they're smack in the burgeoning Internet of Things world. Couple this with the promise and excitement of augmented and virtual reality, the availability and accessibility of drones, robots, and coding classes—it's no wonder Gen Z is dubbed the Maker Generation.[5]

---

[3] Ibid.
[4] Ibid.
[5] Ibid.

Generation Smarts: Working with Gen Z Clients

Generation Z is already showing the world their propensity and talent to create. They represent 20 percent of the population of the United States.[6] Gen Z, not the Millennials, are poised to be our country's most diverse generation. They are the children of the 400 percent increase in multiracial marriages within the last 30 years and among them, Hispanic teenagers are the fastest-growing demographic in the United States.[7]

Their creativity, size, and coming of age at a time of soaring innovation are small hints of the way that Gen Z will change the world. We need to pay attention and engage with them now.

- From a financial perspective, Generation Z faces similar concerns as Millennials. Generation Z faces high un- or underemployment, high student loan debt, and the high pressure of knowing that their financial security will depend largely on their independent efforts (not existing social systems).
- The sharing economy, so popular with Millennials, may be challenged by Gen Z. For example, Generation Z demonstrates a very high desire for home ownership. A recent study shows more than half of teens offered to give up social media for a year and do double the homework if it guaranteed home ownership in their future.[8]
- While they are among our youngest clients and prospects, Gen X thinks about and is engaged in their financial health. A recent study showed their top financial concerns are affording college (39 percent) and having a large student loan balance (39 percent). This concern may have been inherited from their parents, as 58 percent of Gen Z parents surveyed said they borrowed money to pay for college and 43 percent are still paying them back. Perhaps in an effort to spare their children a similar burden, the same study showed that more than half (51 percent) of those parents have arranged a 529 College Savings Plan.[9]
- Developing and offering financial literacy programs to this population will be critical, and it is our obligation. Generation Z developed poor financial habits early. More than half the respondents in a recent survey carried a credit card balance for six months or longer (only 23 percent pay it off

---

[6] http://blogs.wsj.com/moneybeat/2015/12/02/7-things-goldman-says-investors-should-be-thinking-about/.

[7] See Note 4.

[8] http://time.com/money/3318389/home-ownership-generation-z-millennials/.

[9] http://s1.q4cdn.com/959385532/files/doc_news/research/Gen_Z_Release_FINAL6.20.pdf.

each month). Most do not have checking or savings accounts. In addition to your efforts to educate, like the Millennials before them, engaging their parents is a solid strategy. Those Gen Zers who demonstrated good budgeting skills was on account of regular and informative discussions with their parents about saving money (67 percent), compared to those who aren't good budgeters (34 percent).[10]

Paying attention to the changing demographics around us informs so much about our political and economic futures. It is critical to understand these trends from an investing and client-relationship-building perspective. As we wrote this chapter and flowed through the demographics, we have no doubt how difficult it is to run a business keeping five generations (and soon more) in mind. But there are firms that even conceptually are understanding the shifts taking place and adapting their businesses accordingly. Like William Gibson famously said, "*The future is already here—it's just not evenly distributed.*" The most thoughtful and successful investment firms will always have an eye on the future and be looking to build client experiences with the flavor of that future into their processes as a matter of course—not just keeping up.

---

[10] Ibid.

CHAPTER 9

Investing Women

Female Investors at a Glance

Women are not a niche. They are 51 percent of the population and there are niche markets within the women's demographic. Developing market segments of your female clients can take a number of forms. Here are some suggestions for the ways that you can relate better to your female clients. It will be more meaningful and create a better client experience, if you use a "segment". Consider categories such as these suggested here:

- Lifestyle. The following factors affecting the investing needs of women:
  - Age, generation, or phase of life
  - Profession (working outside the home, stay at home, career specialty or industry)
  - Life partner status (single by choice, married, widowed, divorced, same sex)
  - Geographic location
- Behavior and attitudes. Discuss the following with your female clients as you work together to develop a plan for your advisory relationship:
  - Degree of tech savviness and communication preferences
  - Advice orientation
  - Alignment with the way you manage your business
  - Common sets of needs (sandwich generation, elder care)
- Financial and economic factors that affect the client-advisor relationship:
  - Available assets to manage
  - Total income
- Portfolio complexity and risk tolerance

Working with Female Clients

Considering the unique needs of women beyond their gender is a first step. For some advisors, this will be a large change in thinking about and understanding their client experience.

Combining Gender and Generation Smarts

The Center for Talent Innovation's (CTI) Power of the Purse[1] study demonstrated the continued disconnect between women and their financial advisors. The study found across all age and wealth bands that 67 percent of women feel misunderstood by advisors or that their advisor is not interested in them.

This is fascinating when you consider the value proposition of most advisors includes the promise to listen closely and value each relationship. As with most things in life, there is usually plenty of responsibility to go around when a relationship is not working.

Women may feel too intimidated or too detached from their finances to invest in making their needs known and clear, and then holding the advisor responsible. To bridge the distance in any relationship only takes one party to be willing. In the case of the female investor and her financial advisor, the onus rests on the advisor to look for evidence that the relationship with his or her client is satisfying, trusting, and growing.

We find one of the reasons advisors do not engage with and regularly reflect on the relationships they have with their female clients is bias. Too many advisors remain shortsighted and often dismissive of the opportunity female investors represent and they tend to overlook critical facts.

Women Are More Than Wives and Widows

They are significant wealth creators in their own right. Pershing's study *Women Investing with a Purpose* found these significant proof points that demonstrate the economic prowess women investors have and are accumulating

---

[1] Sylvia Ann Hewlett et al., "Harnessing the Power of the Purse: Female Investors and Global Opportunities for Growth," Center for Talent Innovation, May 2014. Available at: www .talentinnovation.org/_private/assets/HarnessingThePowerOfThePurse_ExecSumm-CTI-CONFIDENTIAL.pdf.

quickly. Women are more educated than ever and their earnings are steadily increasing. From the study, consider this:

Rising up in Education: Highly Educated; Highly Paid
- Women with high incomes are very likely to be college-educated—93 percent of women with annual household incomes over $200,000 have a college degree.[2]
- Women are now as likely to have graduated from college as men are—32.0 percent of women aged 25 and over and 31.9 percent of men have attained a bachelor's degree or higher.[3]
- The millennial generation of women in the workforce will be even more educated. In 2012, women between 25 and 32 were 23 percent more likely to have a bachelor's degree than men in their age group.[4]

Rising up in Work: More Opportunities; Earning More
- Today women constitute 57 percent of the total U.S. labor force.[5]
- More working moms than ever before: the proportion of married mothers who are employed, with children, is 67 percent.[6]
- Working moms earn in proportionate levels to their husbands. Married and working mothers who earn more than their husbands has increased from 4 percent in 1960 to 15 percent in 2011.[7]
- The salary of a working woman remains 82 percent that of the average working man's,[8] *but* encouraging statistics show the younger, more educated Millennial generation women earning nearly as much as men. In

---

[2] Spectrem Group, "High Income Women Investors," 2014.

[3] U.S. Census Bureau, https://www.census.gov/content/dam/Census/library/publications/2016/demo/p20-578.pdf, www.census.gov/hhes/socdemo/education/data/cps/2014/tables.html 2014.

[4] Pew Research Center, "Pay Gap, Millennial Women Near Parity—for Now," December 11, 2013. Available at: www.pewsocialtrends.org/2013/12/11/on-pay-gap-millennial-women-near-parity-for-now/.

[5] U.S. Department of Labor, https://www.dol.gov/wb/stats/stats_data.htm, www.dol.gov/wb/stats/recentfacts.htm.

[6] U.S. Department of Labor, "Employment Characteristics of Families Summary," http://www.bls.gov/news.release/pdf/famee.pdf, www.bls.gov/news.release/famee.nr0.htm.

[7] Pew Research Center, "Breadwinner Moms," May 29, 2013. Available at: www.pewsocial-trends.org/2013/05/29/breadwinner-moms/.

[8] U.S. Department of Labor, "Labor Force Statistics from the Current Population Survey," 2013.

2012, among workers aged 25 to 34, women's hourly earnings were 93 percent those of men,[9] and single, childless women in their 20s outearn men by 8 percent in metropolitan areas.[10]

Rising up in Leadership: Leading More; Owning More

- With only 14.2 percent of women occupying the top five leadership positions at the companies in the S&P 500, we still have a long way to go as a society and throughout many industries. But that is not holding women back or their increasing influence in the fabric of America's business. As of 2014, there were about 9.1 million women-owned businesses in the United States, employing 7.9 million people and generating $1.4 trillion of revenue.[11]
- While the numbers are exciting, the big opportunity for advisors is to consider the need these women have for financial advice for themselves and their businesses.

Rising in Influence: Deciding More; Investing More

- While women may not have always had the significant wealth and spending power available to them today, they did seem to have a high degree of influence on household spending, and it continues today with women estimated to control roughly two-thirds of annual spending in the United States, which adds up to about $12 trillion. In a 2013 survey, 75 percent of women reported that they feel responsible for day-to-day household spending.[12]
- When it comes to making decisions about their individual or family finances, women are playing a leading role. Ameriprise Financial released a study, *Women and Financial Power,*[13] that revealed:
  - ○ Fifty-six percent of women say they share in making financial decisions with a spouse or partner.
  - ○ Forty-one percent said that they will make financial decisions on their own. What's interesting is that 37 percent of this cohort are in long-term

---

[9] See Note 4.

[10] Matthew Rousu, "Childless Women in Their Twenties Out-Earn Men. So?" Forbes .com, February 24, 2014. Available at: www.forbes.com/sites/realspin/2014/02/24/childless-women-in-their-twenties-out-earn-men-so/.

[11] American Express, "State of Women-Owned Businesses Report," 2014.

[12] Hillard Fleishman, A Study of Women's Lives, Lifestyles and Marketplace Impact. 2013.

[13] http://newsroom.ameriprise.com/news/ameriprise-study-reveals-more-women-are-taking-command-their-finances.htm.

relationships—and still making independent decisions that affect their financial well-being.

o The study also showed that women across generations are demonstrating more accountability and responsibility in understanding their financial situations, and surprisingly, the group who positively resonates with this statement the most are older women: 91 percent of Baby Boomer women, 84 percent of Gen X women, and 80 percent of Millennial women.

These are all positive signals that should help open advisors' eyes to the new face of the female investor and the potential she has, particularly as she continues to rise in the ranks and enjoy greater pay parity with her male counterparts and continued influence on critical decision making at home.

With this knowledge more ingrained in their client experience, advisors can begin to consider other topics and concerns that are often on the minds of their female clients. These ideas are important no matter what her life stage is and will generally increase your odds of retaining this important relationship with her and ultimately the next critical one—the one with her children. Here are three tools you can use when determining the optimal client experience for your female clients and to start to gauge her satisfaction and loyalty to your firm. The three tools are: the relationship test, gaining a firm understanding of her risk tolerance and risk-taking preferences, and helping her find her purpose.

Now, we will discusses how each of these can be used to help meet client needs in the modern world of investing.

The Most Important Question

While things are certainly changing, many advisors' primary client relationship, particularly in the Boomer or Mature generation, continues to be with a male head of household. While advisors are much more aware of the need to see their relationships not with an individual, but with the entire family, much more work still needs to be done. To help advisors understand how secure their relationship with *her* is, we like to pose this simple question. *"If something happens to* him, *will* she *call you?"* In the more than 50 workshops we have conducted with advisors, we opened with this question. Consistently, only about a quarter of the room, when thinking of their most critical relationships, felt they could unequivocally say *yes!*

Even those advisors who raised their hands, when probed, confessed to us they had some doubt. Recognizing the vulnerability, many advisors, upon returning to their office, questioned themselves and their staff to shore up any weak links or blind spots in the relationship that might evoke a shadow of a doubt.

We then ask a delicate follow-up question. We ask how many advisors have lost a female client after the death or divorce of their primary and male head of household client. Each time, nearly every hand goes up. What was surprising is that the advisors we work with are not rookies! The advisors attending these workshops were often part of President Club trips or Top Advisor conferences, working for many years and managing significant amounts of money. Generally, more than $10 million.

These advisors tell us that when they lost *her* as a client, it was because that important first call went to other trusted advisors and confidants—a family member, accountant, attorney, or another trusted resource to whom she is more connected—and this person, after assisting with the first priorities in those situations, for example, managing the funeral or recommending an attorney, was also there to help with the next most important priority, dealing with the financial impact of either situation, and was also quick to recommend someone to provide financial advice and guidance during these stressful times.

If you're willing to reflect deeply on the relationships you have and want to keep, we find the answers to these questions are always profound and offer advisors some great places to grow and improve their services. *Our most committed clients take this exercise a step further and use it to assess the quality of their relationships with the couple's children, should something happen to the parents.*

Help Her Understand and Define Risk

In one of Pershing's most recent papers, *Women: Investing with a Purpose,*[14] we see that women's financial influence is stronger than ever. More women are using financial advisors, and those who do report high levels of satisfaction and trust.

This study showed that women have the same financial priorities as men—retiring comfortably, maintaining their current lifestyle, and covering health care costs for themselves or family members—but are not entirely confident they will reach their goals.

The lack of confidence may be driven by the unique challenges women face that men do not—statistically they live longer, earn less, have less in savings, and incur higher medical costs. We see one of the biggest opportunities

---

[14] Pershing, "Women: Investing with a Purpose," 2015. Available at: https://www.pershing .com/_global-assets/pdf/women-investing-with-a-purpose.pdf.

for advisors to help women is to bridge an important disconnect between these future realities and many women's current investment risk posture. We think it's a misnomer to presume that all women are risk averse, when in fact it may not be that women are risk averse as much as they are risk aware.[15] This manifests itself in many ways, including women wanting to check things out a little more deeply. Think of buying a new home. A man sees the house once or twice and can usually be fairly comfortable with the decision to move forward. The woman researches the neighborhood, drives it at night, talks to friends, and visits the local schools. She often needs more conviction than a man does when making decisions, and in some ways wants to make a more perfect decision.

She is often thinking about who else will be affected by her decision. How does this benefit not only her, but her children, her family, her life goals—and she thinks through pessimistic scenarios if it does not work out.

Some of the financial advisors we work with receive this information that she has a lower risk tolerance and sometimes make recommendations for lower risk solutions—only on account of this perceived comfort or bias that they suspect.

When we work with advisors, we work hard to help them embrace the concept of risk awareness, not risk aversion, and then spend time with women to answer these questions, plan out a scenario, and develop education and investment strategies to support the women clients. Some of the educational programs we provide advisors help them interact with their female clients on the topic of risk. These programs help them address their clients' deepest, and often unspoken, concerns. These include questions around issues like: Will I outlive my savings? Will my children be cared for and how can I ensure that I will not become a burden to them? After a divorce or death, can I maintain my standard of living?

Here's the thing that financial advisors need to work on to help their female clients understand. Risk management is bigger than the known risks. There are the known risks of an untimely death of a spouse, accidents, and health issues. We can plan for those with tools like wills, estate plans, and insurance. But many advisors fail to talk to their female clients on another dimension of risk—including the risk of not taking enough risk with her investments to receive a return adequate to mitigate the possibility of outliving her savings.

---

[15] Holly Buchanan, "Are Women Risk Averse or Simply More Risk Aware," June 17, 2014. Available at: www.marketandselltowomen.com/are-women-risk-averse-or-simply-more-risk-aware/.

Advisors and their female clients need to push past pure bias like women are risk averse and work to develop their risk management strategies and coach women on risk awareness in a way that is responsible and allows her to mitigate concerns like outliving her savings, or at least the liquid component of her assets, through a thoughtful investment strategy.

Advisors who tap into these often unspoken emotional needs and introduce the topic of risk management as a means to offer women the protection strategies they often seek will have an advantage.

For example, beyond the savings versus longevity issue, women have higher chances of long-term illness than men,[16] yet are often underinsured. One study found that only 18 percent of high-income women report having a long-term care policy, whereas 27 percent of all other investors do.[17]

When meeting with your female clients, one suggestion is to help them bring up these unspoken needs and then focus the conversation on meeting them rather than just on the investments. Taking a needs-based approach is helpful for framing the majority of your financial planning conversations with her. It's particularly helpful for the risk discussion, too.

Pershing's study, *Women: Investing with a Purpose,* shone a light on this fact: When high-income women are asked what might cause them to consider switching advisors, 38 percent of them specified "advisor does not understand my risk tolerance," while 30 percent of all other affluent investors felt the same way. The study suggests that what women are reacting to is not risk per se, but having an aversion to short-term losses.

Their discomfort with short-term loss has 35 percent of high-income women in the study noting that consecutive losses over a two-year period would be a reason for them to consider changing their advisor, and 24 percent of all other affluent investors replied the same way.

Risk doesn't always mean loss, and female clients will benefit from time spent with you to understand the risks of not taking the appropriate levels of risk and see how your guidance and thoughtful planning can help female clients see that too-conservative an approach might undermine their life goals.

Help Her Find Her Purpose

Many advisors believe they are meeting their responsibility and providing an important service when they deliver sound financial advice and investment

---

[16] Canadian Women's Health Network, "Chronic Disease: What Do Sex and Gender Have to Do with It?" 2012. Available at: www.cwhn.ca/en/resources/primers/chronicdisease.

[17] Spectrem Group, "What Bothers High Income Women?" 2014. Available at: http://spectrem.com/Content/high-income-women-bothers.aspx.

options to their clients. We would submit that there is more, and for many women the more is in helping her to achieve her goals and ensure alignment between her investment management strategy and the strong sense of purpose she desires as part of the difference she makes for her personal legacy.

The women surveyed in Pershing's paper *Women: Investing with a Purpose* identified four examples for her life goals that matter more to them than looking at their financial achievements through the dimension of performance returns alone. The four pillars of purpose the study identified are: a secure retirement, ensuring the education of their children and grandchildren, having financial flexibility to pivot their life as they need or circumstances change, and leaving a legacy to the charities they believe in and beneficiaries they want to support through their investment strategy.

Education

Nearly every woman would tell you that if she could ensure one thing, it would be her children's health and happiness. A body of research exists today that points to education and knowledge as critical determinants of long-term well-being, self-determination, and self-sufficiency.[18] Education can help people create a fulfilling life, choose a profession, and build confidence and broaden their perspectives of the world. Seeing one's children acquire the skills and credentials needed to be self-sufficient and a livelihood is top of mind for many parents and grandparents, and women in particular.

This is important to most parents and mothers, but perhaps those with a high degree of education in their own right feel even stronger about it. Pershing's paper *Women: Investing with a Purpose* shows 47 percent of high-income women are concerned with financing their children's education, while only 25 percent of all other affluent investors indicate concern about this topic.

College funding and specialized or graduate education after that is a cause most mothers are eager to fund. Providing education and opportunities are often available as a result, creating a strong emotional desire in women. Many women are willing to extend themselves financially or by working longer to help their children. If this is the case for your female clients, it is important that you work with them to consider how stretching to fund their children's education could create a negative foreshadow on their retirement savings and goals.

No matter what her financial circumstances, be sure to devote significant time to ask her questions about college for children, her goals, and savings

---

[18] Measure of America, "Health, Education, and Income: The Basic Building Blocks of a Good Life," Social Science Research Council, 2016. Available at: https://www.measureofamerica .org/health-education-and-income-the-basic-building-blocks-of-a-good-life/.

plan to get there. We have found a positive in asking women about their children's education plans as part of each meeting. In many client meetings of traditional families, it is often the woman who is forthcoming not only in planning for educational expenses, but alerting the family advisor when school is over, and the $30,000 to $50,000 a year that was going toward financing school is now available for reinvestment.

There is no shortage of investment solutions designed to help fund a child or grandchild's education; what will resonate strongly with most women is your understanding of her priorities and your ability to help her envision, quantify, and financially prepare to achieve her goals—which often begin with her children.

Flexibility

If we were to play a game of word association and said "flexibility" in a conversation about women, the association that might most quickly come to mind is often about her experience in the workplace. For the past 10 years or so, women have been busy trying to advocate for and acquire flexible employment arrangements to help them feel both productive and successful at work and able to provide the level of caregiving they desire at home.

When it comes to their financial priorities, many women are looking for flexibility in different ways. Pershing's *Women: Investing with a Purpose* study found that women seek a kind of breathing room with their finances.

Today, women are acutely aware of the ways they could experience a serious disruption in their lives and subsequent financial setback. These unfortunate scenarios can include divorce, early death of a spouse, a job loss—and other matters that are beyond their control.

Sixty-six percent of caregivers are female. She is on average 49 years old, caring for her 60-year-old mother who does not live with her. She is most often married and employed.[19] This scenario points to the strong possibility that it will be your female clients who absorb most of the pressure when it comes to caring for their children and older parents.

The tension between raising children, caring for parents, and trying to manage their careers often leaves women feeling that they have to make impossible trade-offs. Women have a propensity to put family first, and as a result, she can easily spend a decade or more out of the workforce. These big gaps in her working years, coupled with well-documented less pay, fewer promotions,

---

[19] Family Caregiver Alliance, "Women and Caregiving: Facts and Figures," February 2015. Available at: https://www.caregiver.org/women-and-caregiving-facts-and-figures.

and other workplace challenges, can put many women at a disadvantage. The disadvantage relates not only to her ability to achieve her retirement number but also to create ongoing job security or keeping up her skills and contributions so she's top of mind for recruiters, has a rich network, is movable, and other factors that make it possible to compete for new and upward positions.

Helping her to create and enjoy the freedom that comes when one has a financial cushion is important to women. It makes it easier for her to say yes to a lot of things, including caring for her children or parents, as needed, the ability to seek new and interesting work challenges that excite her, such as pursuing an entrepreneurial ambition, and not having to make money be the primary objective of her employment decisions.

Another major reason for women's desire for greater financial freedom is the reality of divorce and the complications of blended families that often follow. In the United States today, 40 to 50 percent of marriages end in divorce, and the percentage is even higher for subsequent marriages.[20] In the case of divorce, women want to know that they will be okay, that they can continue to maintain their standard of living and not feel the pinch.

When they anticipate second and third marriages, many women are taking precautions such as pre- and postnuptial agreements, or using trusts to secure their financial security and that of their natural children.

Understanding the prevalence of divorce should be on the minds of advisors, not only because it is on the minds of their clients, but because there is a tendency of women who divorce their husbands to leave the couple's investment advisor behind as well.

This is common with widows, too; the studies show mixed results but very often women have little loyalty to their deceased husbands' advisors. Some statistics cite more than 70 percent of married women leave their financial professionals within a year of their husbands' deaths.[21]

What Advisors Can Do

Treat Her as an Individual, Not a Niche

Think about the phase of life your female clients are in and try to anticipate what her needs may be, then confirm them with her. For example, since

---

[20] American Psychological Association, "Marriage & Divorce," 2016. Available at: www.apa .org/topics/divorce/.

[21] Tracey Longo, "The Emerging Profile of Women Investors," *Financial Advisor*, August 1, 2008. Available at: www.fa-mag.com/news/the-emerging-profile-of-women-investors-1961 .html.

family caregiving most often falls to women, many clients will be thinking about their futures as well as those of their parents or children. When working with single women clients, see what's on their minds. You may want to explore their tax situation and offer strategies to help them close the gap in what they may pay as compared to their married counterparts. If *her* parents are still alive, be sure to ask questions about not only the financial demands she may have assisting with elder care, but the emotional and physical ones as well. If she has children, talk to her about the challenges she may face, either emotionally, for example, balancing her child care responsibilities with her work demands, or the financial, saving for college or paying private schools and nannies.

When your clients are part of a couple, there is a lot of valuable conversations you can have there as well. You can certainly focus on any of the issues we've covered, including generational caregiving responsibilities and how the couple will face these emotionally and what the impact may be on the couple's earning and savings abilities. You can work through estate planning and talk about the difficult questions that relate to survivorship, wills, and trusts. Asking provocative questions and providing scenario planning in the form of what-if questions is important. Ask the questions that are on her mind and that both members of the couple should be thinking about regarding a wife's ability to sustain short-term financial stability if the husband should die, for example.

Also when working with couples, don't forget the potential you have to help them strengthen their relationship. Money issues can play a substantial role in why a couple decides to separate.[22] Your expertise can be incredibly valuable here as the combination of your experience and wisdom can help your clients see the emotional needs and fears that often manifest as money troubles in a relationship.

Some of these issues may be around control. When one partner makes more than the other, the higher-earning individual may feel the right to have more control over household spending decisions. Some individuals feel guilt about their spending—and are programmed by lingering family belief systems. When we work with advisors, we found this to be a consistently exciting and important "feel good" moments for advisors. Advisors express a very high feeling of satisfaction when they realize they can help their couples reduce fighting and stress at home by helping them understand their values

---

[22] Geoff Williams, "Why Couples Fight about Money," *U.S. News and World Report,* June 17, 2014. Available at: http://money.usnews.com/money/personal-finance/articles/2014/06/17/why-couples-fight-about-money.

about money, question ingrained thinking or patterns, and then see meaningful change not only to their financial profile but to their overall marriage happiness.

Consider Offering New and Differentiated Services

The pressures women face moving in and out of the workforce, balancing child care and elder care, have highlighted the need and opportunity to guide your female clients through these changes. Many progressive advisory firms now offer services to assist their female clients in these key areas, including:

- **Career counseling and life coach services.** Many advisory firms are considering hiring experts who are capable of guiding their clients not only through life transitions and changes but helping them gain skills and offering workshops on topics that include salary negotiation and ways to find their purpose and passion.
- **Elder care.** Progressive firms are also understanding the value of providing insights and understanding to help clients understand not only the aging process but their options for funding it and living it in a way that is in accordance with how they are comfortable. While it may be initially that your Boomer clients are interested in these services and knowledge for their parents, many will come to appreciate this kind of advice for themselves. Consider hosting events or "bring a friend night" on topics like Social Security, strategies for retaining and remaining in your primary care residence. Help clients decide and understand the implications of long-term health care.
- **Services to help families understand the meaning of money and wealth.** Whether it is helping your couples understand what drives them about money or helping their children to understand the meaning of the wealth they will inherit, these are valuable opportunities to provide basic and more sophisticated financial literacy education programs. For women who have not historically been in charge of their finances and now, on account of a death or divorce, find themselves in this situation, offering to sit with these clients monthly for statement reviews, budgeting exercises, and to build their confidence is a wonderful and appreciated client engagement tool.
- **Help female clients think of their savings as an investment "bucket."** Behavioral finance shows us that investors may be able to commit more to and feel good about their savings plan when they align *what* they are saving for with the investing strategy. Pershing's *Women: Investing with a Purpose* study found that women in particular, when given the choice,

like to structure investment and savings into buckets or pools for a specific purpose. Financial advisors are taking advantage of this and helping their clients set up the typical buckets like retirement, college, and home savings, but also those that help women to save not merely for their own security but for the well-being of others.

- **Focus on solutions and benefits, not products.** When working with your clients, begin with the benefit gained, not the solution or product itself. See the case study about an advisor, a client of ours, who was working with a couple.

Case Study

An advisor began working with new clients, a married couple.

This was a second marriage, blended with children from previous marriages. To build the plan, the advisor referenced the usual assumptions as well as the information provided by the couple.

When it came time to present the plan, this advisor did not start with or provide lengthy descriptions about complicated products like specialized trusts that could be helpful in meeting their needs. Instead, the advisor spoke to the couple's intimate concerns and questions. Using caring language and generous listening, he help show that he could provide peace of mind and answers to their most personal needs. Things like: How can we protect our children's inheritance and still ensure the surviving spouse is cared for and can stay in our primary residence?

Only when this understanding was established did the advisor begin to talk about and offer investment and estate planning solutions.

This turned out to be a very important moment in the advisor-couple relationship. While communicating the benefits of certain product solution was important, what was much more critical was to demonstrate how deeply the advisor understood the heart of his assignment: Minimize potential financial entanglements and keep the peace among family members.

There are many strategies and best practices for working with your female clients. Help them manage their fears and risks of the things that keep them up at night. These fears are often unspoken like the fear of running out of money or becoming a financial burden to one's children. While other female clients are wealth creators in their own right, few advisors are proactive to help them discover wealth-protection strategies or offer business insights to grow their businesses into the future.

The bottom line is whatever you can do to help your clients, especially your female clients, feel more comfortable with their future and not paralyzed about what-if scenarios is a lasting value proposition and a solid foundation to build your relationships.

Unique Planning Needs for Women

For female clients, funding a secure retirement is like swimming upstream. Policy, social, and financial issues complicate the way and there are many factors that must be carefully planned for to avoid undermining her financial health, particularly in her later years.

Pershing's *Investing with a Purpose* study identified six truths that create a particular challenge for women. Each one is an important implication to address in a woman's financial plan. These include:

- Longer average life expectancies—Women have a longer life expectancy than men.
  - Women who reach age 65 are on average expected to live 2.3 years longer than a man who reaches the same age.[23]
- Lower incomes during working years—Men's earnings grow twice as fast as women's.[24]
  - Women earn 79 percent of what men were paid, or a gap of 21 percent.[25] Over the course of a lifetime and with all the competing interests for a woman's spending, this can have a significant and negative impact on retirement security.
- Gaps in employment—Women may take off some time to care for aging parents or others.
  - Many working women are the designated go-to person, or often feel they have no choice in being the primary caregiver to children and/or their aging parents. Women, more than men, often feel that to meet these responsibilities, they will be required—of their own accord or their

---

[23] Social Security Administration, "Calculators: Life Expectancy," 2015. Available at: www.ssa.gov/planners/lifeexpectancy.htm.

[24] Eric Morath, "The Gender Pay Gap Widens and Men's Earnings Grow Twice as Fast as Women's," *Wall Street Journal*, October 20, 2015. Available at: http://blogs.wsj.com/economics/2015/10/20/the-gender-pay-gap-widens-as-mens-earnings-grow-twice-as-fast-as-womens/.

[25] American Association of University Women (AAUW), "The Simple Truth about the Gender Pay Gap," Spring 2016. Available at: www.aauw.org/research/the-simple-truth-about-the-gender-pay-gap/.

employers'—to work fewer hours, decline promotions, or leave the work-force altogether to manage their family and caregiving responsibilities.[26]

- Lower savings levels—Women tend to have lower account balances than men.

  ○ This becomes a grave challenge because women who retired in 2012, as an example, are expected to spend 15 percent more time in retirement than men (20.5 versus 17.9 years).[27]

- Higher medical costs—Women have a higher chance than men of being affected financially by chronic or terminal illnesses.

  ○ This is particularly crippling when you consider that women pay more in average annual health care expenses than men do.[28] Some women will have to make terrible trade-offs, including tapping resources reserved for other purposes in order to fund their health care costs. Over time, these kinds of unpredictable and unplanned expenses, combined with an over-all prolonged life span, can place pressure on an adequate, never mind generous, retirement savings plan.

- Higher taxes—Single women can pay more in taxes over their lifetimes than married couples.

  ○ Over her lifetime, a single woman can pay as much as a million dollars more than her married counterparts for health care, taxes, and more.[29] This is troubling for a host of reasons, including how many Americans are choosing to remain single as a lifestyle.[30]

- Liquidity challenges—Surviving her spouse is not the only challenge that women will have as they approach or live in retirement. There are specific financial and emotional challenges that she may not comprehend, includ-ing the risk of reaching retirement with her "number" intact, but finding those assets, mostly illiquid and tied up as value and equity in her home—difficult to liquidate to maintain her lifestyle.

---

[26] OWL, "Issues: Economic Security," 2016. Available at: www.owl-national.org/pages/issues-economic-security.

[27] OECD, "Expected Years in Retirement," *Society at a Glance 2014: OECD Social Indicators* (Washington, DC: OECD Publishing, 2014).

[28] Agency for Healthcare Research and Quality, Total Health Services-Mean and Median Expenses per Person With Expense and Distribution of Expenses by Source of Payment: United States, 2012. Medical Expenditure Panel Survey Household Component Data. Gen-erated interactively (June 9, 2016).

[29] Lisa Arnold and Christina Campbell, "The High Price of Being Single in America," *The Atlantic*, January 14, 2013. Available at: www.theatlantic.com/sexes/archive/2013/01/the-high-price-of-being-single-in-america/267043/.

[30] Nora Daly, "Single? So Are the Majority of U.S. Adults," PBS.org, September 11, 2014. Available at: www.pbs.org/newshour/rundown/single-youre-not-alone/.

This has financial and cash management implications. It also has emotional implications. Today's retirees are reluctant to leave their home.[31] There are a number of reasons driving this trend. Some are emotional. The memories and feelings of security that being in one's own home can conjure up financial security, some retirees believe, to be less expensive in a home whose mortgage was paid off many years ago than renting or other options available.

It's a fact that cash can get tight for the surviving spouse, especially those who outlive their life expectancy, and selling one's primary home is often the least desirable option. This is when solutions to help retirees stay in their homes are interesting and may deserve a second look.

---

[31] Nanci Hellmich, "Retirees Embrace Ways to Stay Put, Age in Place," *USA Today*, April 2, 2015. Available at: www.usatoday.com/story/money/personalfinance/2015/04/02/homes-of-the-future-for-retirees/24710737/.

PART III

Bringing Change to Your Practice

CHAPTER 10

Transforming from Practice to Business

Elite advisory firms distinguish themselves in many nuanced ways. But there appear to be three big areas in which the top-performing advisory firms (Leading Firms) have made the right decisions that helped them to truly stand out: human capital management, technology implementation, and profitable pricing.

These insights were revealed in "Mission Possible IV," which Pershing commissioned the consulting firm FA Insight to research and write. FA Insight tracked the individual performance of advisory firms between 2008 and 2012, and then segmented the Leading Firms based on growth rate, profitability, and owner's income as a percentage of revenue. The top-performing firms grew revenue at twice the rate of their peers![1]

Each of the Leading Firms demonstrated a level of courage and confidence that was not apparent in the rest of the advisory population. Consider where we were as an economy and an industry in 2008 and how far so many firms fell in terms of assets under management, revenue, and profitability. While there were many advisors who believed this downdraft was an aberration and eventually the markets would reinvigorate their businesses, the Leading Firms in this study went a step further by actually investing ahead of the curve while also adopting better discipline around technology selection, profitability management, and people recruiting and retention.

---

[1] https://www.pershing.com/our-thinking/thought-leadership/mission-possible-iv.

One data point that reveals this newfound discipline is that for the Leading Firms in this study, their overhead costs (expense ratio excluding professional compensation) decreased to 36 percent of revenue. Meanwhile, the overhead expense ratio for all other independent advisory firms rose to 45 percent of revenue in 2012.[2] A 9 percent variance is huge. For example, if your business generated $2 million in annual revenue, you would be spending $180,000 more on overhead than a comparable Leading Firm.

One consequence of better expense control is that the Leading Firms produced an operating profit of 29 percent in 2012 compared to 13 percent for the rest of the industry on average.[3] For a $2 million practice, that variance means the Leading Firms had an operating profit of $580,000 compared to $260,000. What I like about this statistic is that it validates the argument that people are an asset on which to get a return and not just a cost to be managed. Clearly, the investment these firms made in human capital paid off.

When surveyed in 2009, almost half the advisory firms that have emerged as the Leaders said they intended to add head count and were not planning to lay anybody off. For the most part, they made good on this commitment with the median firm adding two more people for every half-time employee by the average firm.

This reveals a keen understanding by the Leading Firms as to what ultimately drives growth in the advisory business. The reality is that most advisors suffer from limited capacity, which makes it difficult to pursue or even take on more clients without materially altering the client experience or terminating existing clients. By investing in capacity before their growth occurred, these Leading Firms were in a better position to take advantage of market movements and the addition of new clients who had become alienated from their previous financial advisor during the downturn.

A subtle shift in who these firms hired also occurred. Instead of perpetuating the old approach of hiring other advisors or "rainmakers" who may or may not work out, these firms added so-called nonprofessional staff at a lower cost but with superior administrative skills so that their current team of business developers and advisors could become more productive and effective.

As an example, lead advisors have been able to increase the time they spend with clients to 75 percent compared to 52 percent for the average firm.[4] This increased capacity frees them up to take in even more clients

---

[2] Ibid.
[3] Ibid.
[4] Ibid.

without affecting the experience. Furthermore, the revenue per professional in the Leading Firms is $150,000 greater than in the average firm.

It is no coincidence that these fast-growing firms also added professional management, which also freed up the advisors to focus on new business opportunities and existing clients while still executing on their business plan.

One area in which professional management contributed greatly to the Leading Firms was in how these firms deployed their technology. By realizing that what matters is not the number of tools used but rather the way in which technology is used, these professional managers introduced disciplined selection processes, emphasized training, and focused on improving workflow efficiencies. What is interesting is that while the Leading Firms showed better profitability and productivity numbers, they spent less of their revenue on technology than the average firm in the study.

In addition to leveraging technology to improve their business-to-client processes, the Leading Firms tended to use technology more effectively to monitor and troubleshoot service delivery. Nearly 70 percent of the Leading Firms use time-tracking, CRM, and project management software in their business today.

The other area of business discipline that professional managers brought to the Leading Firms was around pricing strategies. Obviously, 2008 and 2009 tested the mettle of all advisors, particularly with respect to their client relationships. Many firms discounted their fees, waived minimums, or avoided fee hikes because they were unsure of how their clients would react. Many were humbled by the market cataclysm and to a degree lost belief in what they were doing was adding value.

Once again demonstrating a contrarian's courage, the Leading Firms decided not to compete on price but on value, recognizing that they truly earn their keep in the most difficult of times. In the spirit of calculated aggression, many moved toward premium pricing. By commanding a fair price for value, they not only showed confidence to their clients, but they were able to cull out those clients who did not perceive the advisory relationship was worth the price.

Leading Firms were most aggressive with larger clients with fees on $5 million portfolios being raised by 10 basis point on average, while the other firms in the study reduced their fees by 10 basis points on average for comparable clients. A roughly similar trend occurred on assets above $10 million.

In addition to raising fees on their largest clients, the Leading Firms also strictly imposed fee minimums. This helped avoid the perception that large clients were subsidizing smaller clients and ensured that the smaller clients were paying fair value for the advice they were getting. It also ensured that they were able to cover their costs of serving lower-value clients.

Business owners, just like investors, make calculated guesses every day with the hope of a better payoff. In the case of the Leading Advisory firms, they clearly made decisions informed by the facts and were not swayed by emotions. They positioned themselves well for a strong market upswing, and to capitalize on the new business opportunities that would eventually come their way.

They have blazed the path for others who may be more timid about their growth strategies. Obviously, the Leading Firms made choices when the world was in a trough. Much has changed since the Great Recession began, but the argument for hiring ahead of the curve, deploying technology more intelligently, and maintaining pricing discipline still makes sense for growth-minded advisory firms.

But Are You Scalable?

Common wisdom holds that the advice business is not scalable. While operating leverage may be easier to attain in other industries, such as manufacturing or software development, advisory firms can achieve scale once they reach a certain level of critical mass.

Investopedia defines a scalable company as one that can "improve profit margins while sales volume increases."[5] Does that description apply to advisory firms?

The 2014 *Financial Performance Study of Advisory Firms* conducted by *Investment News* and sponsored by Pershing Advisor Solutions revealed that many growing advisory businesses are seeing margins improve as revenues increase (see Figure 10.1). For example, overhead expenses as a percentage of revenue dropped from a high of 48.1 percent to 28.9 percent as advisory firms broke through certain revenue and asset barriers.[6]

The most precipitous decline in the expense ratio was noted when advisory firms became "Super Ensembles," defined as an advisory business with at least $10 billion in assets under management (AUM) and at least $10 million in annual revenue (see graphic).

For the average independent firm, these numbers may seem daunting, but $10 billion of AUM is not beyond the reach of the next generation of

---

[5] Investopedia, "Scalability Definition." Available at: www.investopedia.com/terms/s/scalability .asp.

[6] *Investment News*, "2014 Financial Performance Study of Advisory Firms," October 19, 2014. Available at: www.investmentnews.com/section/specialreport/20141019/FPSTUDY.

FIGURE 10.1 Crtical Mass

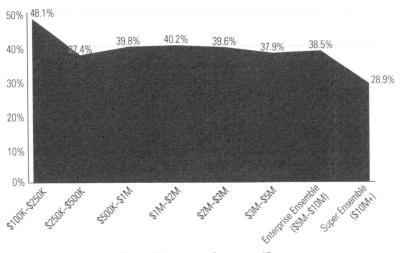

■ Overhead Expenses as a Percentage of Revenue

Source: 2014 *Investment News* Financial Performance Study of Advisory Firms

financial advisors. Not only does the expense ratio decline as a firm gets bigger, but revenue growth also accelerates with size. Why? Because a larger market presence creates increased efficiency, stronger discipline around business development, and the ability to build a brand.

The number of Super Ensemble firms today proves that the business of financial advice is going through profound change. When Mark started benchmarking the profession in the late 1980s, many advisors hoped to get to $100 million of AUM. At the beginning of this decade, the new Holy Grail was $1 billion. Now, the many firms breaking through the $5 billion mark and even the $10 billion mark reveal a transformation that few could imagine when the independent advisory movement took root.

Yet most advisory firms are small businesses that suffer the same strains as any closely held enterprise. The Small Business Administration defines a small business operating in the service sector as a company with revenues no greater than $21.5 million.[7]

The consolidators like Focus Financial and United Capital are capitalizing on the travails of running a small business by bringing like-minded firms together under one company, and new model firms such as Hightower are creating national advisory brands using broker-dealer command-and-control

---

[7] https://www.sba.gov/contracting/getting-started-contractor/make-sure-you-meet-sba-size-standards/summary-size-standards-industry-sector

structures while delivering an advisory experience. But sizable owner-operated enterprises like Silvercrest, Aspiriant, Oxford Financial Group, and Tolleson have redefined the way advisory firms look and feel by growing strategically and organically, and not necessarily through aggressive recruitment or acquisition models, though tuck-in mergers may have rounded out some of their growth.

The achievement of scale provides a clear economic advantage to advisory firms. It enables such businesses to be more effective at the recruitment and development of talent without straining the income statement, it helps them to create critical redundancies, and it allows them to compete on price in cases when that is important.

There are risks to growth, however. The pursuit of critical mass can also contribute to cultural dysfunction, defection of employees, and impaired quality control. The more the principals in a firm are removed from the daily activities and supervision of specific client engagement, the greater the risk that steps may be neglected, recommendations may be inappropriate, and errors may be made.

To protect against self-destruction brought on by growth, advisors must view scale not as a natural byproduct of growth, but as something that occurs only when the leadership is thoughtful about the business they wish to create, systematic in the processes they implement to manage growth, and aware of the metrics that indicate when their train is going off the rails.

Advisors must focus on the following key areas if they hope to achieve scale:

- Expansion into new locations
- Examination of workflow and processes
- Recruitment, retention, and development of people
- Constant monitoring and measuring of critical ratios

We cite expansion into new locations first because this seems to be the way in which advisors believe they can grow quickly—by merging in or acquiring another firm in a different city. The first question one should ask is whether the firm can achieve critical mass in the new location itself. Based on our experience, it appears that a reasonable level of operating efficiency occurs when an advisory firm generates in excess of 10 million of annual revenue (a proxy for staffing, assets, and clients in most cases). At this level, an advisory firm has sufficient redundancies and capacity to grow. When advisors open an office in a new location with no plans to get it to critical mass, they become vulnerable. The loss of a key client or key employee or partner in the remote location may force them to close up shop as quickly as they opened the doors.

Streamlining workflow and processes probably constitutes the easiest way to manage growth. Most advisory firms have been doing the same thing the same way since they began. When they reexamine their approach, they often discover many functions that are repeated over and over again and therefore could be automated or done by a lower-level associate in the firm. An improved workflow enables advisors to lower their cost of labor and increase their efficiency, both of which help to reduce operating expenses within the firm.

Talent retention and development may be the area of greatest risk. All businesses tend to lose some focus as new people join the firm. To counter this, firms must implement a conscious strategy around training and inculcating the values that leadership holds dear. Regular performance evaluations and meetings with new associates help to reinforce expectations. When the advisory firm opens a new location, the ability to transplant cultural values becomes an even greater challenge if a culture carrier is not deployed to the new office. A decision on whether to merge, acquire, or open a new location may hinge upon whether the firm has somebody willing to relocate to provide this necessary leadership.

As with any investment, it is important to define success and to measure performance against those metrics. Even more critical is the need to establish leading indicators for the firm in general as well as for all branch offices or divisions. In addition to tracking operating profit margin and gross profit margin, it is helpful to monitor other ratios such as clients-to-staff, revenue-per-staff, revenue-per-client, error rates, growth rates, and attrition rates.

It seems likely that the advisory profession will soon resemble the accounting profession, with a small number of national firms, a larger number of regional and local firms, and the smallest number of solo practitioners. While the advisory business in general is profitable, there comes a point in the life cycle of a firm when its owners have to commit to growing or to staying small. Those caught in the middle never achieve scale or operating efficiency because they are too big and too small at the same time.

Fortunately, current models of success demonstrate how larger enterprises can not only grow efficiently, but also serve their clients effectively.

Risky Business

Someday soon an advisor will have to declare bankruptcy because he or she will not be able to cover the losses incurred in a fraudulent third-party wire transfer or a money laundering scheme. We don't know who and we don't know where, but I'm absolutely certain that the attempts to defraud are challenging the way in which advisors are managing risk.

Sometimes this occurs because advisors mistakenly believe that their broker-dealer or custodian is responsible for preventing the fraud. While such firms play a role by providing surveillance and tripwires that stymie illegal transactions, the ultimate burden is with the advisor, particularly those who are serving in a fiduciary capacity. It is not a responsibility that advisors can abdicate.

Independent advisors who have been given discretion over client assets and who have power of attorney to move money on behalf of their clients are especially susceptible. Those associated with a broker-dealer have the capital protection that comes with this affiliation, though even that could be inadequate to cover the loss if their BD is a small, lightly capitalized business. RIA firms, on the other hand, have no capital requirements so any losses would be debited to their management fee account or they would be required to pay out of their own pocket for any losses their clients incur.

Readers may be wondering why an advisor is on the hook for a crime committed against their client by someone else? The principal reason is that they are the ones responsible for verifying whether the request to wire funds is legitimate, they are the ones who send the instructions to the broker-dealer or custodian to execute the wires, and they are the ones who are responsible for KYC—know your customer.

They are also the ones who get most exasperated when the broker-dealer or custodian (when they smell something fishy) slows up the wire request. The advisor often argues loudly and sometimes profanely that "the client said he needs the money, so just send it to him!" In many of these cases, the aggressive advisor claims he confirmed the request with the client when upon investigation of the fraud, the custodian finds out he did not—because he did not want to bother his client or he was too busy. The only thing less defensible than carelessness is dishonesty.

More often, the advisor is fearful of looking unresponsive and in some cases unsympathetic when the wire transfer takes more than a few hours, so they put pressure on the keeper of the assets to act with alacrity. Sometimes, advisors also get touchy when the custodian elects to contact the end client directly to reverify what the advisor said was legitimate.

The Setting

Every day, sophisticated criminals from Detroit to Dubrovnik are capturing personal information on your clients, including e-mail addresses, financial data, copies of previous correspondence, and copies of signatures and account numbers. They are on a relentless campaign to take your clients' money.

Often they begin with an innocuous request to the advisor asking about the available cash in the account. In some clever cases, they will add the balance inquiry to a previous string of e-mails so it appears like ongoing correspondence between the client and advisor. In a typical "e-heist," the fraudster sends an e-mail to the advisor requesting money be transferred to a third party. It is often colored with some type of inconvenience that suggests it is hard for the client to be contacted. This would typically be something like, "I'm at a funeral," "I'm traveling where there's no cell or Internet service," or "I'll be in meetings all day and need to get this done in order to complete an important transaction."

Eager to demonstrate good service even when reacting from the golf course or the beach, the advisor or his staff responds by sending the Letter of Authorization (LOA), which is signed and returned. What the advisor or her staff may not realize is that while the e-mail address used by the perpetrator may be legitimate, it is also a hacked account to which the fraudster has direct access. Absent any protocols by the advisor, this is as easy as lifting a wallet from an open handbag.

When the fraudster returns the signed forms to the advisor, he in turn forwards it to the custodian or broker-dealer for processing. With this authorization on file, the custodian conducts some safety checks to see if there are any anomalies or inconsistencies, and then wires the money to a third party as instructed. Those funds are immediately rewired to a bank in Malaysia whose offices are already closed for the night so nobody working in such locations can stop the fast-moving money from going out again. Those funds are moved quickly from the foreign account in the form of a debit card or cash withdrawal and the money is gone forever.

The bad guys are master manipulators who can use different forms of layering to cover their tracks. For example, they will troll dating websites to recruit unsuspecting accomplices. These unfortunate and oftentimes lonely souls are commonly referred to as "mules" who in the course of the seduction give up their bank account information as part of their Internet relationship. The fraudster will create a story about why he can't take the direct wire and will ask his new romantic interest to accept the deposit of $50,000 to her account, for example. He will then direct the unwitting accomplice to Western Union, to send $45,000 to him and keep $5,000 "for when we meet." When contacted by law enforcement, the accomplice will honestly be oblivious to what just happened and explain she was only effecting this transfer at the request of her "boyfriend."

The Response

Four things can help to stop frauds like this:

1. Train your staff on the red flags.
2. Check to see if there were recent changes to their profile records.
3. Always use the phone numbers and e-mails on file to respond to requests.
4. Always call to verbally verify the request.

There are some common clues that you are about to be hustled by a fraudster. For example, when a request for a third-party wire transfer is inconsistent with the client's past activity, you need to confirm that the client is in the loop. You can also find clues in the content of the requests when there are spelling and grammatical errors, or the requests are too formal. The requests often contain an explanation of how the funds will be used, such as the purchase of furniture using funds in an IRA, or tuition payments when the client doesn't have school-aged children. We saw one request for the purchase of commercial baking equipment, which if for no other reason, stirred the advisor's curiosity to inquire directly with the client.

To set up the transaction, a fraudster will often send instructions earlier to have the phone number changed. This way, when the advisor or his staff calls to confirm, they may not realize they are actually talking to the thief and not the client.

Avoid responding directly to the e-mail or phone number they provide. They may make a subtle change in the e-mail address and set up a new account that the advisor directs the response to, beyond the view of the legitimate client. For example, they may remove a period between first and last names, or eliminate a letter in a long surname so it looks correct in a cursory review. They also will say they are unavailable at their home or office and direct the advisor to call an unfamiliar number. The advisor or her staff may not know the client's voice so these tactics can work.

The advisor or his staff should always call the client on the numbers on file to confirm the request before sending out any forms. In the event the forms go out and are signed and returned, the advisor or staff member should compare the signature to other legitimate documents and look for other inconsistencies in the request. The job of confirmation is often left to an administrative person. As part of your training, they have to know that avoiding the call or ignoring the protocols is not excusable. In one example, a fraudster sent an e-mail saying he couldn't talk because he had laryngitis. Believing that that was reasonable, the advisor's assistant did not make the call and the client's funds were gone in an instant.

Vigilance is the duty of everyone in financial services. But clients themselves can do more to protect their data and information from the evil eyes of conniving spies. The next area of added value for advisors may be education programs and lessons on encryption to ensure that clients get not only a return on their money, but a return of their money. That said, it's rare that the investor is not made whole by the advisor, custodian, or broker-dealer. The question is whether those covering the losses have the financial wherewithal to withstand such pain.

The Price of Independence

Semantics are important. For example, when one refers to oneself as an independent advisor, does this mean he or she is an independent business owner; independent in the ability to select technology and platforms; independent in ideas and recommendations to clients; or independent from direct supervision?

The answer to this question becomes important as financial advisory firms become more complex and new opportunities for conflicts and confusion arise. Furthermore, with each new innovation and each new claim of fraud or malfeasance against financial professionals of all stripes, clients and regulators are demanding more transparency into all our business activity. The more there is a quid pro quo element to your professional relationships, the less one can hold oneself out as independent by any definition.

Holding oneself out as independent does not in itself connote a higher standing or a better business model, but it is often expressed in a self-righteous tone. So naturally it begs the question: "What do you mean by independence?"

Thus, our challenge: We are an industry that uses garbled language to convey images to less-informed consumers and so it becomes more difficult for them to tell the difference between a zebra and a horse. Is business ownership and governance your definition of independence? If yes, then at what point in your growth cycle and span of control do you no longer have independence? If you have multiple partners, each of whom has a say in business governance and policy, have you drifted away from the freedom to act according to your instincts or own ideas? Do you lose independence the bigger you become and the more shareholders you accumulate? It's a bit like asking, "When does a boat become a ship?"

If you sell your firm, are you as free to conduct your business as you did when you were not owned by a passive investor? Are there consequences for not hitting your growth numbers and does this influence your behavior? If you become a division of a bank or an accounting firm, do you have the freedom to make decisions that make sense for your advisory business but which conflict with the policies or interests of your parent? If independence means freedom to use whichever vendor you want whenever you want, how in fact do you demonstrate that, and how do you communicate this value to your clients? For example, if you are in a referral program with your custodian, and they require that in return for the lead you must hold those assets with them and pay them a referral fee in perpetuity, are you selecting the custodian based on the client's best interest or yours? How do you communicate to your client what limitations (or increased fees) this program may impose on their assets over the life of the relationship? And if you decide the custodian is no longer delivering on its promise of good service or high value—or is still a safe place to hold your assets—may you move your clients without consequences to them or you?

If they give you favorable pricing in return for your use of their proprietary mutual funds, ETFs, or cash sweep accounts when they make substantially more in the relationship with you, are you giving your clients access to the whole of the market as a proper fiduciary advisor? Or are you acting as a salesperson for their products? If they give you money for technology or some other business support at a ratio tied to the volume of business with you, are you free from conflict?

If independence means you are free to make investment recommendations or act with discretion, how does that affect your independence when your broker-dealer limits you to only those solutions in their proprietary managed account platform? If your firm requires that you use only the master limited partnerships sponsored by your own company, are you acting as a client advocate or product advocate? If you are dogmatic users of ETFs or index funds and unwilling to consider other investment vehicles, are you truly independent in your advice or tied to a specific type of product?

When was the last time you truly analyzed the relationship between your firm and its vendors? How do these relationships affect your firm's independence? How does this trickle down to other decisions your firm makes?

An even bigger question is why do firms enter into agreements with others knowing that they will be giving up a portion of decision-making control?

Is it due to budgetary concerns? Lack of resources? Miseducation? Unavailable internal resources? Industry pressure? What can we do to remove these barriers and allow growing firms access to technology, vendors, and products that do not create such conflicts?

As the definition of independence can be somewhat blurry, how do regulators like the SEC enforce disclosures of conflict of interest?

We're sorry for asking so many questions, but there are compelling reasons to probe more deeply into the subject for advisors, custodians, and broker-dealers.

In particular, several issues have arisen lately that contribute to these blurred lines. The first is the push by many in the profession to have all people delivering financial solutions to act in a fiduciary capacity. The second is the Department of Labor's insertion into this debate on behalf of all retirement accounts, including IRAs. The third is the advocacy by groups such as SIFMA, FSI, and FINRA to adopt a harmonized fiduciary standard that protects their constituents but may not be consistent with how RIA firms currently interpret the guidelines. The fourth is the rapid consolidation of the industry, the emergence of more corporate buyers, the expansion of the hybrid advisor movement, and other factors that scramble the distinction between a broker and an advisor.

Before these forces of change, life in financial services was much clearer to consumers, regulators, the media, and even other people in the profession. There was a time when a broker was different from an advisor, when "fee-based" and "fee-only" did not imply the same thing, and when advisory firms were all owner-operated. But since circumstances have changed, we need to rethink the language we use to describe what we do and the intent with which we do it.

The confluence of these issues makes the definition of independence a sentence constructed of only dangling participles. What does the adjective modify? Business model. Ownership. Advice. Choice.

Why Does the Definition of Independence Matter?

The business model under which one operates is supposed to clearly reflect what clients should expect of you. A broker has a different obligation to a client than an advisor, for example. If my body aches, I want to know if I should be going to a chiropractor or an orthopedist. If my vision is bad, I want to know if I am seeing an optometrist or an ophthalmologist. If I am seeking tax advice, I want to know if I am seeing a CPA or an enrolled agent. Who you are helps to convey to clients a clear idea of what you do and how you do it.

This is not to imply that one business model is superior to another, but if how we conduct our business is not obvious and transparent to the client, then the integrity of our profession takes yet another hit. The overuse of the word "independent" is a good example of a simple phrase that tends to confuse the masses.

Are You Conflict-Free?

One strong magnet for the advisory side of the business is that one becomes a professional buyer versus a professional seller. The implication is that when acting as a client advocate instead of a product advocate, you are able to clearly position yourself firmly on the side of your clients. Clearly, one of the most appealing position statements in financial services is to profess a freedom from conflicts of interest. However, positioning oneself as "conflict free" may be the most difficult to prove. Regulators are poised to raise the bar on the fiduciary standard even higher.

In particular, the U.S. Department of Labor's (DOL) regulation of the retirement business will clamp down on advisors who seem to serve their own interests before the interests of their clients. The DOL's emphasis on a fiduciary standard of care likely will apply to the general delivery of advice in all of its manifestations, not just retirement accounts.

Acting in a client's best interests is always the proper stance. Can you imagine a doctor proclaiming disdain for the Hippocratic Oath, which requires physicians to swear by certain ethical standards? Yet how are these standards defined in the financial services arena? The DOL's proposed guidelines identify an ethical tipping point in the payment of commissions to brokers who sell financial products.

The DOL seems to view the payment of commissions as self-dealing and conflicted, as advisors may be incented to trade to generate income. They believe that conflicts may be mitigated by contractual obligations that will create a higher standard of client care. Pressure on the industry is causing many to shift to an advisory, or as some broker-dealers term it, fee-based model to diminish the threat of self-dealing.

Registered Investment Advisors (RIAs) who are fiduciaries under the Investment Advisors Act, and probably already act as fiduciaries under ERISA, are thrilled to point out how their fee-only approach positions them as client advocates rather than product advocates. Consequently, they feel validated by the government's efforts to control conflicts of interest in the professional management of retirement savings.

Many contend that "what's good for the client is good for the profession" and assume that there is enough business to go around. However, before RIAs become too self-righteous about their business models, this community must examine its own conflicts.

If you accept dinner with a fund company or tickets to an event from a technology provider, does this create a conflict? If you accept a referral from your custodian in return for keeping the assets on their platform forever, are you acting in your client's best interests—or your own? If you charge fees based on the amount of assets a client brings, are your interests truly aligned? If you talk your client out of paying down their mortgage and thus keeping more assets under your management, do you disclose how this benefits you?

One of the greatest conflicts we see in financial services occurs when the client pays a fee based on the value they bring instead of the value the professional offers. How does a person's net worth dictate the amount they should pay? That is like a doctor charging by the pound. In this comparison, both professions would be equating size to complexity, and the amount accumulated (in dollars or pounds) to the effort needed to serve the client.

The entire financial services industry is in dire need of a reputational facelift, but the new regulations raise some important questions about how the business of financial advice will be conducted post implementation. It would be a mistake for RIAs to think that a new fiduciary standard for the management of retirement accounts will not influence their business, including the vehicles they use such as options and derivatives; differentiated fee-based pricing for equities, fixed income, and cash; or even actively managed mutual funds. If there is a massive shift to passive investment vehicles, will active managers provide enough thrust to lift the indices that the passive vehicles depend on?

More clarity is required but I see two separate government agencies with two different definitions of fiduciary standard: one being a rule and one being a guidance policy. This will create complexity for RIA firms including new compliance standards, new tests for managing certain assets, and perhaps new certifications and examinations to ensure the business is competent and compliant.

Up until 1998, with a short interruption imposed by the federal government, motorists were allowed to drive on Montana highways at the speed limit of their choice as long as it was reasonably prudent. As soon as they crossed into Idaho or Wyoming, they had to adhere to the 55- or 65-mph speed limit that governed drivers in those states. Montana said, "Use your judgment as to what's reasonable and prudent." The other states said, "By law, we will tell you what's reasonable and prudent."

In this comparison, Montana's system represents the fiduciary standard under the SEC, while the standard under the DOL resembles Idaho's law-based approach. How will you govern the fiduciary behavior inside your firm? Will the new standard cause you to change your strategy for going under the radar?

These questions are all academic at this point, as we don't know how clients, advisors, and supporting organizations will adjust their ways of doing business for the long term. We can assume that the push for greater transparency, fewer conflicts of interest, and more complete disclosures will improve the behavior of those motivated purely by the sale of a product and instill more faith and confidence in this industry. We will also likely see an even broader shift to retainer fees, hourly charges, and other relationships that better align advisors with the value they deliver.

CHAPTER 11

Culture Wars

There are transformative events in every business that imprint an indelible mark on employees, clients, and vendors. The way in which each of these parties is treated will cast your image as either a mercenary or a missionary.

In this context, a missionary is someone who has a strong belief in what they are doing and why they are doing it, and will strive to convert people to their way. A mercenary, on the other hand, is one who is acting or doing something purely for money.

Now we recognize the danger of segregating an entire industry into two overly simplistic categories. Obviously, there are shades of gray. And one should not infer that mercenaries are inherently evil or that missionaries are necessarily good. They are just propelled by a different kind of fuel. Simplicity in this case allows you to examine whether you are creating the environment you admire and desire, or whether you are encouraging a different way of acting by your partners, clients, and associates.

For example, companies that value production over all else encourage mercenary behavior. So too do organizations that consider shareholders more important than clients or employees. Firms that have an overly stingy attitude about expenses and resources would also fall into this category. The common denominator is that all behavior in these cases is driven by immediate financial results tied to short-term acts.

Those who behave like missionaries tend not to be "me-first" or "money-first" types. They are more inclined to think of others first, especially their clients and employees, before inquiring about cost or return. Their inclination may be toward a longer-term payoff because they believe by doing the right thing, their rewards will eventually come. It's not uncommon to find recovering mercenaries in this group because they have made enough money to feel like they can afford to be more generous in their behavior, but at their core they may still ask how much something costs or how much they can make.

While both types can be successful in business however you define success (profits, growth, value), their approach clearly dictates the culture they will ultimately create. The best of these firms have a healthy balance between financial reward and doing what's right. The worst of this lot are those who preach commitment to clients, employees, and family but in real life make decisions primarily for the money. The world hates hypocrites whether in religion, politics, or business, so mercenaries posing as missionaries present a dangerous threat to the health of any organization.

Mercenary businesses are compelling to some because their owners and top producers can achieve great wealth quickly. But they are vulnerable to high staff turnover, low morale, increases in client complaints, fraud, and other forms of malfeasance.

Many argue persuasively that this is how the country's largest banks and brokerage firms contributed to the Great Recession. Companies that become large and unwieldy must manage to the lowest common denominator and oftentimes that means filtering every decision through revenue, cost, and profits. These metrics are simple to measure, the levers to pull are obvious, and shareholders can easily relate to decisions viewed through a financial prism. With a heavy tilt toward generating financial returns no matter what, the stewards of these firms lost sight of what mattered most.

The new model advisor seems to find the missionary model more compelling because it focuses less on sales and more on advice. The risk to firms drifting too far in this direction is the failure to recognize the need to manage to profitability and hold people accountable for results. Missionary models oftentimes overcustomize for clients and overaccommodate for staff, which is agony for those who are high performers.

But many studies validate that organizations that are in tune with the needs of their employees and clients first tend to be higher-performing businesses over the long term. For example, in studies that Pershing has sponsored and Moss Adams has conducted, we found that niche-focused advisory firms that build a value proposition around the requirements of a particular set of clients grow three times faster than the average practice. By comparison, the underperforming firms that tended to have more of a product focus (meaning a focus on what they sell versus who they serve) lagged behind those that were geared to the needs of a specific client community.

Advisory firms organized around a mission or purpose to profoundly affect the lives of others also tend to serve as a sort of spiritual guide to those working in the business. For example, there are several firms that select clients on what they intend to do with their wealth rather than just a desire to get richer. For employees of advisory firms, we have found that money by itself, over time, does not have the same type of sustaining motivation that personal growth opportunities and career advancement have of helping others. Money can provide a short-term boost to employee productivity, but it's more like Red Bull than a healthy, well-balanced meal. That said, without a fair and appropriate reward aligned with the behavior you seek, even missionaries can become disillusioned.

Conversely, it takes a long time to detect how short-term decisions for financial gain impact the long-term health of an enterprise, and how the behavior of its leaders result in converting missionaries to mercenaries. This is often the unintended consequence of making finance the sole filter for business actions. When employees see how the company makes its decisions, they tend to behave in a way that is valued by the firm regardless of whether it reflects their own set of beliefs. As a result, short-term positive financial results encourage leaders to double down on the strategy regardless of the long-term impact of how clients and employees feel about the company. Like Pavlov's theory of behavior, every time someone rings the bell, these leaders begin to salivate. Once caught in this eddy of money, it's hard to extricate the business from what it has become. Meanwhile, those with a missionary mindset tend to get frustrated by the disconnection between what they value and what the firm leaders are doing.

But to think this is a big company dichotomy is wrong. The same behavior found in large banks and brokerage firms sits within Main Street advisory practices. We've often heard advisors say something to the effect that if you want something done right you must pay for it. We've always questioned the logic of rewarding people for doing the right thing. How far have we descended when every action must be impelled by a financial reward? When did we as an industry become a kennel of Pavlov's dogs?

There is one absolute truth about working in financial services. If you are good at what you do and the marketplace recognizes it, you will make a lot of money, certainly more than a large percentage of the population. The question is whether this gets you to where you want to be as a business. Does it allow you to create an enterprise with lasting value that is an employer of choice for the right kind of people? If yes, that makes each decision you make much easier. If no, what will you do about it?

Many firms that have a mercenary culture thrive at least for the short term. But there is a preponderance of people who choose not to operate in this environment because it emphasizes revenue production over all other values. The first and most important question to ask when assessing the culture you have created is: What do you want your business to be known for to both employees and clients?

There are two experiences that cause people in this business to be exhilarated: when you land a big new client and when you hire a great new talent. While the loss of a client can create the opposite emotion, the loss of a key colleague has a way of bursting your balloon completely.

This is especially true when that person is part of your succession plan. There are countless stories about people in this business who have groomed somebody to eventually take on their role, but as the transition slowly begins to take root, the successor departs. The alchemy of turning what should be a natural process into a valuable and sustainable transformation is the elusive holy grail of hiring and retaining people.

Advisory firms often seek our help when managing through major events in their life cycles. We recall being asked by a mid-sized advisory firm for help on their succession plan. There were three current partners and six partners-in-waiting, or at least that's what the owners thought. When I met with the nine of them together, the first question I posed to the non-partners was, "How many of you would like to be an owner of this firm?" None of them said yes. Imagine the shock of the three original partners! When I probed further, the six said they enjoyed their current work and life balance, but they did not relish the risk of being a partner and did not have any ambition to be seen as one.

While their decision is not the same as a defection, it is a reflection of the mindset that many key employees seem to have when operating in an entrepreneurial environment. People you value may view their work with you as a job while others view it as a career. Whether voluntarily or involuntarily, you will eventually experience turnover in your business. Your challenge is to sort out those who are committed to your mission, your purpose, and their own progression as much as you are.

Such experiences are the flotsam and jetsam of business life. Those who have managed for any period of time will see those cast overboard float by in different careers, in different jobs, and in different companies. People coming and going are as natural as sunrises and sunsets, but far less pleasurable.

Clearly, the job of attracting and keeping good people is a chemistry experiment. People join companies for myriad reasons but seem to leave them for just a few—culture, mismanagement, pay, or a true desire to do something else somewhere else. This is where the chemistry comes in.

For years now, we have preached the belief that if you provide each employee with a compelling future, opportunities for growth, a positive environment, and a fair reward, that you will ensure your legacy through the individuals you hire. For the most part, these are elements you can control. The uncontrollable elements reside in the individual him- or herself. It's hard to know what demons are whispering in their ears about whether they feel worthy for the job they are being asked to do, or whether they are feeling appreciated and valued, even when you think you are going out of your way to acknowledge them. It's also hard to know what family pressures they are experiencing, like marital discord, dysfunctional children, or anxiety over their personal finances.

One reason often expressed by people leaving one's company is their lack of desire to take on a top executive position because they doubt their ability to lead. Or they see how the stress of that role has played out in the life of the current leader.

The lure of greener pastures is also a hard view to change. Some of your staff may have joined you from other organizations. As their frustrations mount with the way in which your firm conducts its business or their inability to get things done or get the resources they need, they begin to reflect on all the good things they had at their old employer, conveniently forgetting the reasons why they left in the first place. They also compare your company to others in the market that projected an image of career opportunity, unlimited capacity to grow, infinite resources, and rich rewards.

When defections occur, your critics cite your shambolic human capital plan, your lack of empathy, and your failure to provide opportunity quickly enough. While self-reflection is a healthy way to redress your process of hiring and developing staff, it might be even more constructive to develop a process of checking in with people in whom you are investing. What are the signs that this was a crumbling experiment and is there anything you could do in the future to make it work better the next time?

One of the dangers in developing your messaging to the market is that it could express a view not believed by your own people.

We were reminded of this when participating in a meeting in which the partners in the firm stated the number one reason clients chose them is because of their people. Watching the body language of some of the younger employees, I could sense that this might be a discordant note.

Finally, one of the Millennial employees screwed up her courage and spoke: "If it's true that your people are your greatest asset, then what are you doing to demonstrate to us how much you value that investment?" It was a single act of bravery that caused the room to go silent for a moment until one of the partners asked her to explain what she meant.

Nervously, she said that she was happy at the firm but often she feels as if the partners are only interested in how she supports them and not in her career development. There's never a discussion about the areas they think she should work on, or an encouragement to develop new skills or get exposure to other parts of the business. She said that while she and her contemporaries share the same passion for excellence as the partners—and they truly love working with their clients—they also know that this can't be the final stop on their trip to fulfillment.

Obviously, we are taking some liberties with the language she used, but the essence of her message resonated with us. First, never use a positioning statement that is not universally shared by your own staff. Two, never invoke the quality of your people without demonstrating how you tend to their lives, their work, and their careers. And three, if you get pushback on what you think represents your culture, take inventory and then take action to resolve the conflict.

This episode personifies one of the greatest challenges facing advisory firms today. According to Cerulli Associates, there are roughly 40,000 fewer financial professionals in all channels in the United States than there were in 2008.[1] The average age of advisors is also rising.

So naturally, we have characterized the human capital crisis in financial services as a talent shortage but the reality is that we are facing a management deficit. There is a core reason why motivated people fail to join our profession and fail to stay. Our profession's inability to successfully recruit, retain, and develop talent is not just a reflection on the reputation financial services has earned as a bad place to work. That is a contributor, of course. But it's important to recognize that except for the big banks, insurance companies, and brokerage firms, the delivery of financial advice is done substantially through small businesses that operate as Registered Investment Advisory (RIA) firms or through affiliation with independent contractor broker/dealers.

Evidence of this is that since 2008, the captive wirehouse brokerage world has seen its market share drop from a high of 44 to 38 percent today.[2] As a result (or perhaps as a consequence), the big firms have focused less on recruiting new people while instead trading senior experienced people among them. Meanwhile, in 2014, there was an increase of 744 RIA firms.[3] Since the vast

---

[1] www.ey.com/Publication/vwLUAssets/Advice_goes_virtual_in_asset_management/$File/ey-digital-investment-services.pdf.

[2] Michael Wursthorn, "Big Brokerages Hanging On to Their Dominance," *Wall Street Journal*, January 26, 2015, www.wsj.com/articles/big-brokerages-hanging-on-to-their-dominance-1422279743.

[3] www.riainabox.com/blog/2280-new-ria-firms-were-started-from-may-2013-to-may-2014.

majority of these firms are small in relative terms, they are not focused enough to systematically hire talent and develop careers. Many lack professional management or a true human capital executive. So the decision not to hire new people to the business by the big firms and the ineffectiveness in developing talent in the small firms add to our talent challenge as an industry.

The transformation of the business tells us we are at an inflection point. With an oversupply of clients and undersupply of people to provide financial advice, there is an opportunity for financial services firms to truly position themselves as the employer of choice. This can be done on a local level or a national level and it can be aligned with your messaging. To get there, advisory firms need to answer a few tough questions:

1. What does it take to make your people feel engaged?
2. What would it take for your staff to say with conviction that people are our differentiator?
3. What compels people to join our firm?
4. What compels them to stay?

In a way, it's much like developing a strategy to attract and retain clients. But it's an inward focus with the goal of creating capacity, business continuity, and growth. It's a real epiphany when you realize that your best employee is more valuable to you than your best client.

As with investing, a bull market for talent camouflages many sins. But when we are experiencing an acute talent shortage as we are today, it forces firms to develop a true differentiator in the talent wars. Three big areas in which firms need to ramp up their game are in defining and managing:

• The nature of the work
• The nature of the worker
• The nature of the workplace

Nature of the Work

It is common for advisory firms to have job descriptions but they are often written in terms of function and duties. Rarely do they include an indication of what success in the job looks like. While many like to blame younger generations for lacking a work ethic, the number one reason for failure is the inability to match the right people to the right job. The best firms are having no difficulty maximizing the potential of Generations X and Y.

Nature of the Worker

When you have a clear idea of the nature of the work, you should also be able to identify the optimal characteristics of the person filling that job. If the role is repetitive and routine, it will have more appeal to a one-ball juggler than to a multitasker. If it requires a lot of on-the-spot judgment and response such as in client service, you will need to have a process that allows for more autonomy than control.

Nature of the Workplace

The key to creating an environment in which motivated people will flourish is to minimize the distractions, or what some human resource people call dissatisfiers. The idea is that if you matched the right people to the right job, then you want to do all you can to have them focus on their work without things that might frustrate them such as poorly performing technology, a bad boss, a toxic work environment, or even abusive clients.

So ultimately the key to creating alignment between your vision for the business and the people you count on to execute your business plan is to be clear about what you value as an organization. A statement of cultural values is a good place to start, a statement that includes phrases like passion, intellectual curiosity, lifetime learning, leading by example, accountability, and respect.

But having a statement of cultural values by itself is not sufficient. Having both a systematic method of evaluation based on these qualities you expect from everybody is key, both for the employees and the partners. Upstream evaluations of how the partners in a firm treat others provide an excellent coaching moment for even the most seasoned person—even if he or she is the founder. I have yet to meet a person who has achieved perfection in all aspects of his or her life. So having the human capital plan apply to them demonstrates to others the firm's total commitment to the idea that its people are important.

In the end, clients usually do make decisions to work with a financial professional if they are connected to its people. But in today's world, advisory firms have the dual challenge of being attractive to talent as well. Therefore, it is important that one's vision and mission are reinforced by your behavior. A good place to start is with the question: Am I doing all I can to demonstrate that people are our most valuable asset?

Act Like an Owner

One of the most popular reasons entrepreneurs give for not promoting individuals to partnership is because "he or she does not act like an owner." We've long pondered this expression. What does it mean to act like an owner?

The answer to this question was crystallized for us in a discussion at Pershing's U.K. Advisor Council meeting in aptly named Lower Slaughter, a 1,000-year-old town located in the Cotswold district of England. In addition to the usual English and Scottish contingent, several members of our U.S. Advisory Council participated as well. One revelation was that the challenges of running an advisory business were universal, especially when it came to questions around recruitment, retention, compensation, and ownership.

The catalyst for the discussion around what it means to be an owner was a statement by the CEO of a very large advisory firm who said, "Our business is not the same as when our business was founded. We grew but without an organizational chart and performance reviews. Now that we have more partners, more people, and more moving parts, we have to standardize the way in which we do business. We have to balance the wishes of the founder to be entrepreneurial with the needs of the business to develop people and hold them accountable."

In describing the history of his firm, this CEO explained, "When we started this firm, we had to write checks to buy equity. That was a financial strain for many of us, but that is what it requires to create a business. Nobody gives it to you.

"When subsequent employees were invited to become partners, they complained of not having the ability to fund the purchase, so we loaned them the money from the company and issued dividends to help them cover their payments. In a way, it was a riskless transaction for them since they didn't have to pull from their own savings to buy in.

"Some obtained their equity in 2007, the point of its highest value. We lent a lot of money to make this happen. As you can imagine, the valuation declined with the market. When we sold the business in 2010, many of these shareholders were underwater in terms of valuation, just as a lot of people were who heavily mortgaged their homes. They wanted us to write off the loans as worthless."

Asked by the other participants what would he have done differently, he cogently stated three key points:

1. Never give away equity, always sell it—they need to write a check to feel like owners.
2. Remind all partners continuously and repeatedly what the obligations, responsibilities, and liabilities are of ownership.

3. Be more diligent in the evaluation process to ensure that prospective partners grasp the concept of ownership and are willing to accept the risks as well as accept the rewards that come with it.

On this final point, the other participants jumped into the fray. "What does it mean to be an owner?" someone asked.

"If you see something, say something. You have to hold your partners accountable for their commitments. You are responsible for developing others in your firm. You have to make prudent decisions around spending money. You have to speak as one voice to the employees to show we have a shared vision and commitment. You're not an employee anymore, so take responsibility for what you are doing and what the firm is doing."

The exchange of ideas was fast and furious. The essence was that becoming an owner in an advisory business is like becoming a member in an exclusive club. To paraphrase the biblical line, many are considered but few are chosen.

Why? What are the elements that stymie their ambitions to become partners?

Advisors tell us that without a meaningful financial contribution to the business, there is no way that the firm can afford to add someone as a partner. The challenge is how financial contribution is measured. Is it in new business development or client retention? What's interesting is that most advisors generate over 90 percent of their annual revenue from existing clients, so it's always interesting that current owners only value new business development. This is a paradigm that has to change. If associates manage relationships well and obtain additional revenue as a result, isn't this as valuable as attracting new clients?

The answer is partially "yes." If everybody were focused on retention and not new business development, then the advisory firm could not grow fast enough. So the best way to measure financial contribution is a balance of new business and existing business, even if the latter came by virtue of someone else in the firm generating the opportunity.

The second element that limits an associate's growth potential is his or her inability or unwillingness to develop other people. Those who do not help in the development of younger associates are not helping to build a business to last. This next generation will dictate whether the business has a sustainable future. Conversely, if the individual is one who takes credit for everything and does not take the time to teach, mentor, or coach, then he or she is lacking in one of the big characteristics a firm needs in its partners.

Third is their attitude and approach to safety. It's not uncommon for advisors to say that compliance is the purview of the Chief Compliance Officer

(CCO) and abdicate all responsibility to them. In reality, the CCO is not the company cop, but a center of excellence that helps the firm serve its clients with integrity in accordance with the rules promulgated by the regulators. The obligation to operate in accordance with these rules sits with everybody in the firm, especially those who perceive themselves as partners or wannabe partners. But safety is not just an issue of compliance. Client acceptance and retention, behavior in and out of the office, managing to profitability all contribute to the perception of whether one looks like partner material or not.

The fourth element is leadership and management. Lone rangers do not make good partners, no matter how much business they bring in or how many assets they manage. If you accept that partnership is an exclusive club, then you must accept that all the nonpartners will look to you as an example, an icon, an inspiration; someone interested in the careers of others and a commitment to the firm's vision. Leaders are those who can balance strategic and tactical thinking, communicate with clarity, listen attentively, and accept responsibility for their actions. One does not need a title to be a leader and so those who do not qualify to be partners are those who wait to be appointed to something before accepting responsibility to act.

The final element is whether you are likable, a culture carrier, someone who others would want to spend time with. This may be subjective but remember, the current partners are the ones who make the decision about who gets invited in. It's hard to imagine why partners would want to spend any time—let alone partners' meetings or executive offsites—with someone they cannot relate to or even look forward to seeing. This is not to suggest people need to change their personalities, but it may mean they have to do an attitude check to make sure they are not offensive, irritating, or out of sync with the others.

To act like an owner is to recognize the responsibilities that come with it, to act with confidence, to make good and ethical decisions, to hold others accountable, and to contribute in a meaningful way to the organization's success. Seniority doesn't matter. Nor does where you went to university, or where you worked before, or what your current job is.

Bullies on the Job

Have you ever wondered how it is that some people can be charming on the outside but horrible tormenters on the inside? I recall a phrase from a book I read many years ago that referred to these individuals as "charismatic manipulators." In today's parlance, we call them bullies.

A while back, there was a brouhaha in the National Football League's Miami Dolphins in which Jonathan Martin left the NFL football team after accusing Richie Incognito of bullying, which brought this issue to light once again. For the more diminutive among us, it's hard to imagine how a 300-pound offensive lineman could be intimidated in such a circumstance, but the reality is that there are victims and jerks in all kinds of work, and physical strength is often not sufficient to bring the bully down to size.

In fact, in this case, as with most circumstances that involve bullying, harassment is often not physically threatening. It could be repeated unfair criticism, micromanagement, jokes at another person's expense, dismissal of one's point of view, and picking favorites to work with all the time while isolating someone else. The emotional toll caused by bullying undermines the culture of an organization, becomes costly in regard to employee turnover and poor productivity, and is destructive in regard to teamwork.

The financial services industry is filled with workplace bullies. Check out any movie about Wall Street and you will see the stereotype—brash, bold, vulgar, and disrespectful is perceived as the norm. Before Mark moved from Seattle to New York to take on his executive role at Pershing, he said he was warned that these kinds of people would now be a bigger part of his life. It may surprise many that he found New Yorkers to be sometimes friendlier than Seattleites (who, he states, are probably more polite), so thankfully he was not shocked into submission there. In fact, the reality is that the amount of abuse in the center of the financial universe is no more than what I have also witnessed within Main Street firms, which is my point—destructive behavior exists in small towns and big cities, in tiny firms and big banks.

Having worked with hundreds of business owners (including a number of our own partners) over our careers, we've had the distinct displeasure of engaging with scores who use bluster, verbal abuse, intimidation, and manipulation to get their way. Some of us can simply walk away from these relationships when they become intolerable. For most employees and partners, however, to do so is very difficult.

This dynamic seems especially present when other family members are part of the firm. It's not uncommon to see advisory firms founded by dominant personalities turn into hostile environments for spouses and kids. I can recall many circumstances in which an advisor's son or daughter had been elevated in title, but diminished in status when working for their mom or dad. The other employees also see it, and their lack of respect in these circumstances continues a vicious cycle of abuse.

Many advisors I've consulted with in the past about the culture of negativity they are creating were in denial about their own bullying. In their minds, they were "tough but fair bosses."

In his terrific book *How Will You Measure Your Life?*, Clayton Christensen (HarperCollins, 2012) argues that if you hire motivated people, match them to the right jobs, and eliminate the distractions, then you will produce the desired outcome. He said that when these hygiene factors, including status, job security, and work conditions, are not right, they cause people to become dissatisfied. The consequence is an underperforming business in which nobody wants to work.

So here is the question for you: Have respect and good manners begun to slip in your office? Has rude behavior become the norm? Is the biggest perpetrator a partner in the firm? Is there someone else who needs to be put in his or her place?

According to the Workplace Bullying Institute (www.workplacebullying .org/), "bullies often act just under the radar, denying their hostile intent or shrugging off their behaviors as humorous or insignificant. Yet, the constant tension they create—and the way their harmful activities tend to build over time—damages the individual targets of their bullying and the business as a whole."

The WBI explains that workplace bullying . . .

- Is driven by perpetrators' need to control the targeted individual.
- Escalates to involve others who side with the bully, either voluntarily or through coercion.
- Undermines legitimate business interests when bullies' personal agendas take precedence over work itself.

Sherri M. Gordon, the author of *Beyond Bruises: The Truth About Teens and Abuse,* said that workplace bullying is a lot like what goes on in grade schools and high schools.[4] She identified several characteristics to watch for and address:

Verbal abuse. A bullying boss humiliates you in front of others. He also might shout, swear, or yell at you on a consistent basis or make offensive jokes at your expense.

Persistently intimidates. Intimidating behavior might include threatening to fire you or cut your pay as a way to maintain power and control.

---

[4] https://www.verywell.com/signs-your-boss-is-a-bully-460785.

Questions your adequacy and your commitment. Bosses question your adequacy by belittling your opinions and ideas. This may be done in private or in front of others. They also may blame you for problems at work (while claiming that all the good outcomes are due solely to them). And they may question your commitment to the job unless you work long hours and sacrifice personal time.

Undermines your work. Bosses who bully set unrealistic deadlines and change guidelines on a regular basis, causing extra work and increasing the chance for failure. Refusing to provide needed feedback are other tactics used to undermine work.

Impedes your success. Bullies may punish you for mistakes that are not yours or bring up past mistakes in order to shift blame. They also may make it impossible for you to apply for a promotion, a transfer, or additional training. They may even overcontrol or micromanage your work or projects.

Spreads rumors about you. Bullies often go to great lengths to make others look bad. As a result, they may gossip with others about your work, your appearance, your health, or your personal life.

Isolates you at work. Bullying bosses might exclude you socially. They leave you off party lists and don't include you in company outings, sporting events, or after-hours meetings. They also may schedule meetings when they know you have a conflict in your schedule. They may go so far as refusing to allow you to attend work meetings or work lunches.

It's important to recognize that any of this behavior is not a normal part of any workplace environment. Repetitive verbal abuse, exploitation, micromanagement, and other activities that repeatedly demean you will eventually erode your self-esteem and passion for what you do. It will also have a deleterious impact on the business itself, which is why leaders within advisory firms have to take stock of the behavior they tolerate, including their own.

It is the ultimate responsibility of the practice leaders to confront bullies, weed out bad behavior, and create a climate of trust and support. But victims of abuse should not suffer in silence. This only enables bullies to continue their maddening ways. If the business owner is the biggest bully of all, you can enlist allies in the firm who the boss respects to call out improper behavior, or you can make the choice to engage him directly. If the only choice is to seek employment elsewhere, try to avoid making that decision in haste or based on emotion alone, but in a deliberate way to ensure that you leave the firm on good terms and you join the new business with a positive frame of mind.

The Benefits of Reverse Mentorship

One potential failing that comes with age is hubris, a state of exaggerated self-confidence based on believing we have seen it all. As the abridged quote from Proverbs says, "Pride goeth before a fall."

This is a particular challenge for those who make their driving decisions by looking in the rearview mirror. While our history and experience may help us evaluate our circumstances, neither is effective at informing us as to what those circumstances will look like going forward.

Pause for a moment to think about what has changed in financial services in the past 20 years: There has been a massive shift to independent business models away from large employer-based financial services companies; there are far fewer financial advisors; there is an increasing propensity to serve clients by charging fees versus commissions; interest rates have been near zero for a very long time; the average age of a financial professional has crept up closer to what our parents considered the retirement threshold. Add to this the threat of consolidation, robo-advice, and overregulation. The list, of course, is much longer, but the point is we are entering a period of change that many wizened veterans have never seen before.

So while we can rely on our wisdom to process the facts, the circumstances of our current world may require the hopeful view of youth rather than just the jaundiced view of experience. Think for a moment what the landscape will be over the next 10 years: more clients and staff born after 1985; more use of technology to interact with others and to manage our businesses; more transparency into how we conduct our business because of regulation and access.

Of course, the optimal strategy considers multiple points of view so successful business plans won't be one-dimensional. The key based on what are emerging as critical assumptions about the future of our business is to tap into the insight that younger people can provide based on the way in which they live, work, and consume information.

One way in which we at Pershing have begun to elicit new perspectives is with our reverse mentoring program, in which we pair up Millennial employees with our entire executive committee. While the idea of reverse mentoring has been around for years, the application of the concept to our company was developed by our former colleague Gerry Tamburro, who was head of Pershing Prime Services at the time, and two of his Millennial-age employees in, Kayla Flaten and Jamilynn Cimino.

Mark's first reverse mentor was Kayla, but we all agreed after two years it was time to give others an opportunity. He has had two other mentors since then, also from other parts of the business, and in one case, from a different city and state. This is our reality, in which people often work remotely from each other and must find ways to communicate even when our desks are miles apart.

Initially, many of our goals with the reverse mentoring program were to become more proficient with technology, and more informed as to the power of social media. What we found is that this is not just about technology. The most valuable guidance most of the participants say they have received has been around how they interact with younger employees, how to communicate, and what implications the rapidly changing trends have for our business. Most participants say it has been one of the most profound learning experiences they have ever had because it has taken a point of view critical to our future and systematically informed and challenged the way in which they think, act, and resolve problems.

We have heard some folks outside our business say they have children who do the same thing for them, and we have no doubt that that is true. But the dynamics of kids and parents are not the same as mentor and mentee, and that's how the reverse mentoring program has made a difference.

When the task force behind the reverse mentoring program conceived of our approach, there were several elements we deemed as critical:

- The reverse mentor should not have a direct reporting relationship to the mentee.
- Both parties should agree whether they'd prefer an agenda or a more ad hoc approach to discussion—resolve this up front to ensure compatibility of approach.
- The meetings should be scheduled on a regular basis.
- The dialogue shouldn't be limited to the schedule but should be continuous as each party hears and sees things that are relevant.
- Each party should give and receive constructive feedback and challenge each other.
- If the relationship isn't clicking, either party has the right to call it quits.
- Aim to leave organizational hierarchy outside the door; collaborate as equal learning partners.
- Both parties should be explicit about maintaining and respecting confidentiality.

The initial idea was for the mentor-mentee relationship to be in place for one year. In some cases, the connections were so strong that they continued beyond that date. We also found it to be healthy and constructive to switch out of those relationships and introduce new reverse mentors.

Since our reverse mentoring program has become known in the financial services industry, a number of advisors have inquired as to how the idea could be applied within their businesses, particularly since most operate within small firms and the dynamics may be a bit more awkward. To achieve the same success that members of our executive committee have enjoyed with this initiative, here is a plan of action for advisors to consider as you implement your own process:

- Either through study groups, professional or industry associations, or community connections, organize an effort with a group of similar firms that have Millennial-age employees. It is important that the number of participants be manageable at first so you can better evaluate the impact.
- Develop criteria as to which Millennials would be best suited to serve in the role of mentor and nominate them for this project. Criteria should include communication skills, job performance, listening ability, and intellectual curiosity.
- Mutually agree to assign mentors to mentees with pairings that appear to be the most compatible.
- The mentors and mentees should agree on a set of goals and continue to refer back to these goals as the relationship builds.
- The group should collectively create a list of possible topics that should be part of the future agenda as a way to boost the dialogue.
- Ask the reverse mentors to meet monthly to act as sounding boards to one another to discuss topics that came up and share ideas but do not disclose personal or confidential information that was shared by the mentee. Obviously, this is a leap of faith but part of the criteria for selecting mentors is your level of trust and confidence that the individual is discreet.

The risk for those who lead a team or manage a company is that decisions are made without adequate reflection or consideration of critical perspectives. This is not to suggest that consensus building is superior to decisiveness, but ensuring that other critical points of view are considered usually results in a better outcome. A sure way to prick an inflated ego balloon is to be questioned by a younger person as to why we think as we do or act in a certain way.

The reverse mentoring program provides an opportunity to learn from others with whom you might not normally interact at such a deep level.

Furthermore, it has the potential to deliver insight on matters of critical importance to your future clients as well as your future employees and partners.

The biggest testimonial to the power of this program came from my reverse mentor who said, "This has helped immensely with employee engagement, retention, and the mentor's personal development." Most of our reverse mentors say they have become much more confident and learned valuable leadership skills because of this process, which they feel will help their career and our firm.

CHAPTER 12

A Vision and Leader for the Future

The best leaders in the business of financial advice have these five characteristics:

1. Vision
2. Ability to translate vision into action
3. Ownership and accountability
4. Empathy
5. A core belief that their very best employee is more important than their very best client

Don't believe the headlines. It's not just Millennials who are looking for a new kind of leader. Employees everywhere want managers who will listen, consult, coach, and build community over old-style command and control leadership styles.

According to a study commissioned by Pershing, the most popular new leadership quality is someone who inspires innovation through creativity, lifelong learning, and self-renewal. This new style of leadership was preferred over leaders who focus on efficiency by 81 percent of the general public.[1] Leaders who see themselves in service to others were preferred by 62 percent over leaders with traditional qualities of command and control.

---

[1] Pershing, "Americans Crave a New Kind of Leader," 2014. Available at: https://www.pershing .com/_global-assets/pdf/americans-crave-a-new-kind-of-leader.pdf.

Vision: It Begins with Your Guiding Principles

We tend to think of "having a vision" as a tool leaders use to guide their business, to understand where they are going and how they will compete. That is true.

Our work and our personal experience, however, have shown us that before one can truly build a vision for their business, they need to establish a vision for how to live their lives. The behaviors that leaders walk themselves becomes the behaviors expected in the organizations they create. They become the glue, the culture, and the team that creates their success.

As an example, one advisory firm we know well required that all four partners vote on those they were considering as clients. They would evaluate them on how they treated their spouses, what they did in their downtime, how they perceived their last experience with a financial professional, and what their expectations were. It was important in their case that they extend culture all the way through their client experience, which began with good client acceptance in the first place.

It is possible to create successful outcomes without a personal vision, but when leaders take the time to understand and clarify their personal values, their success is supercharged by engaged employees, a team that is diverse in thought and makeup, and a deep understanding of the impact they have on the people around them.

Having a vision for your life is a deliberate undertaking. Take Caroline O'Connell, a senior leader at BNY Mellon. Years ago, at a crossroads for how to build her department and team, Caroline spent a weekend reflecting on what she thought and believed about how a team should form, operate, and define success. By the end of the weekend, not only had Caroline clarified her values, she gave them a distinct voice when she opened her heart to share these with her team through many fireside chats and personal conversations, ultimately going so far as to publish them as her guiding principles.

Caroline did more than share her values. By being willing to stand up for her beliefs, by being open about what she stood for, it was clear to everyone what values would be sought after and which ones would be unwelcome. In doing so, she gave each person in her department an implied and important challenge: Personify these shared values and engage in behaviors that benefit everyone, or enlist her help in finding an environment more suitable to one's personal ambition.

The guiding principles established by Caroline are not platitudes. They govern Caroline's and her department's actions. Caroline set the example and went first committing to these principles. They now inform important decisions about which team members to part ways with and created new criteria for promotion (other than competence and expertise). They inform the interview process for new hires, and understanding these values is critical for new hires to grasp and demonstrate as they onboard.

By having the professional courage to dig deep and give a voice to her values, by patiently teaching others to model these values, by not being afraid to confront incidents that were in opposition to the guiding principles, Caroline personified the adage that people follow first the person, then the plan.

The results Caroline's organization has achieved makes these ideas credible, practical, and worth considering for every organization.

Guiding Principles, Global Marketing and Communications Team

Caroline O'Connell, Chief Marketing Officer, Investment Services, BNY Mellon

1. The quality of the individual is paramount
2. Value creativity and innovation
3. Never rest on the status quo
4. Be an agent for positive change
5. Think strategically
6. Be a strong team player
7. Strive for excellence in all that you do
8. Honor and respect the strengths of each of your teammates

A strong foundation is built when we spend the time to reflect on, clarify, and communicate our personal values. With this first step intact and a team built and motivated by similar characteristics, we can turn our attention to establishing our vision of leadership and ultimately a vision for our business.

It's important not to confuse a statement of cultural values with judgment about what others deem important. Rather, a statement of cultural values serves as a guiding principle for the people you hire, the clients you serve, the partners you choose to work with, and the way in which you define success.

Our Leadership Vision

Establishing guiding principles and a leadership vision are personal and deliberate endeavors. Guiding principles denote the cultural values by which we run our organizations. Guiding principles express the behaviors we will tolerate and reward and which ones we will do without. A leadership vision expresses the heart of what we do and how we will lead.

When we take time to know ourselves and create our leadership vision, we gain a powerful story that inspires those who choose to follow and support our goals. We also gain a deeper understanding of the purpose of our lives and why we have chosen to lead as we do. Our leadership vision becomes a bright North Star, which keeps us on track, guides our behaviors, and establishes a clear *how* for the ways in which we will do our work.

We said that creating a leadership vision is personal and deliberate. It takes courage and effort. There are no shortcuts. You cannot adopt someone else's vision and still be authentic. While there are places to find inspiration, the most conscious and meaningful visions come from our own stories. We all have a story inside of us, but it takes courage to examine it and vulnerability to share it.

Our leadership vision is often percolating in us before we realize it, and it can come from the most unlikely places. Many of us develop our leadership inspiration from the heroes of history and literature. These archetypes can show us how to tap into powerful human qualities such as courage, resilience, and compassion.

Our leadership vision can also be inspired by the adversity we have overcome. For example, a client of ours is frequently asked about what informed his leadership vision. Many of us in this industry want to understand what fueled his path from the small Midwestern town where much of the population lives below the poverty line and it is winter nine months of the year to the leader of a thriving business headquartered in the Northeast.

Colleagues who have been fortunate enough to work with him describe our client as a peacemaker and thoughtful negotiator. He has created opportunities for the people who work on his team and for his clients. He is known for his transparent communications, his unassuming, easygoing nature, his sense of humor, and his professional courage to take on and talk about the hard stuff.

Developing his leadership vision was not the result of time spent with a consultant or coach. It was not the result of reading books or going through a particular exercise. Rather, it was only when he was asked to tell the story of his life did he come to understand the hidden gifts of his trials that later became his key leadership tenets and the core to his legacy.

Our client's early years were filled with adversity. There were many painful moments from losing a parent, having an alcoholic father, and schoolyard bullies. It was nearly impossible to understand or see at the time what skills he was learning while dealing with these childhood stressors. With the gift of hindsight, our client came to see what he was learning was how to face adversity in a positive way.

Little did he know then what a critical skill was developing in him to prepare him for what would come later in his life as he faced the trials many entrepreneurs face, engaging and leading a team, developing people, and the path alone to rise above the negative circumstances of his youth.

As he looks back, he sees that his experience growing up in a poor part of the country with limited opportunity and few role models presented him with a choice: to either accept it as a dead end or to use it as motivation to become better.

While there are other strategies to finding our leadership vision, this man chose one of the most powerful that is available to all of us: using his personal history and life experiences. The power of using our own personal stories is in its authenticity. As a colleague or friend when you hear someone's story, you learn something about him or her. You appreciate the person more as a person and more as a leader. It becomes safe to share your story because they have shared theirs. It is easy to trust a leader like this because what they're asking you to do—in the case of our client, to rise above your circumstances—is not only his words. It is an authentic personal trajectory, walked one step at a time, not something conceptual or out of a book.

What other tools can help you develop your leadership vision? Jim Crowley, chief relationship officer at Pershing, frequently shares a technique he calls establishing a "virtual board of directors." Early in his career, Jim noted the leaders who had qualities he admired. By being a student of these qualities and keeping this group of leaders in his mind, he had a sense of them guiding his interactions, behaviors, and decision making that led him from corporate trainee to having a seat on Pershing's executive committee and eventually becoming their chief relationship officer.

Jim's experience inspired us to counsel others to create their own virtual board of directors. We have found it to be a great mechanism for keeping our behavior in check. Having a virtual board of directors means now, before we send an e-mail or run down the hallway, we can check in and pause. We can pause and reflect on what our internal board might do. Would they send this blazing e-mail? How would they manage conflict? How would they dress or communicate to express their executive presence? It's important to take this pause before moments of joy as well as in the more obvious moments that challenge us. We can also reflect on how our board would guide our celebrations or thank someone for their contributions. Having a virtual board of directors can be a great touchstone in our often-stressful lives to keep us on track and keep us showing up as the resonant leader we want to be.

Let's put this into context. Have you ever been mismanaged? It's important to reflect on this question because the behaviors we learn from others such as our parents, our teachers, or our bosses often predetermine the way in which we relate to our employees. Should we be blind to how our approach affects others, we may also miss the moment that we are about to lose their commitment to our business.

I've heard many old-time managers say about their employees, "They should be grateful I've given them a job. If they don't like it here, they can leave." Or they may add an emotional spin: "I worked damn hard to build this business up. And I did it without complaint. They just have to suck it up if they want to be here."

We suppose that if the financial advisory profession was flooded with talent, we could be this harsh and cavalier about how we are recruiting and retaining staff. But the reality is that there are fewer financial professionals in all channels of this business since 2008. The 100-plus universities that are conferring financial planning degrees say they place most of their students in jobs and have a waiting list of more openings. Every growing advisory firm we meet says they are in the hunt for more talent.

Furthermore, the cost of employee turnover is high. Human resource experts say that it will cost a business somewhere between 150 and 250 percent of a person's base compensation to replace them. This is calculated based on the need to raise salaries to recruit new people, lost productivity, the learning curve for new employees, and in our business, even lost clients.

So it begs several questions: What's the value of being a curmudgeon? How does it help you to view people as a cost to be managed rather than an asset on which to get a return? How much effort does it really take to show people how much they are appreciated and valued? How much benefit can you derive from using mistakes as teaching moments rather than opportunities to punish or rebuke?

While it should be intuitive that one attracts more bees with honey than with vinegar, management behaviors applied over time are as hard to unlearn as any bad habit. Perhaps it's best to begin with an examination of your relationships with key people to determine whether you are close to another lost moment in which they are edging toward the exit or completely disengaged from your business.

More than anything, how your staff relates to you or lives by your statement of cultural values is often based on what they observe, not what they read, or what you say. Especially in times when it's difficult to find qualified people who fit into what you are trying to build, one must be careful not to lead by exception.

We hope it is clear how taking the time to establish a leadership vision and guiding principles can inform your decisions as a leader. When we invest in these tools, we build our business on a rock. What began as a set of beliefs and is now our future and solid results as it manifests. Our leadership vision and guiding principles help us focus on what matters most. We become intentional about what we want to accomplish for ourselves, our teams, and our communities. It is a clear vision and understanding of the kind of leader we hope to be and the legacy we will leave.

Being clear about our values and vision make managing day to day easier and more effective. Hiring is no longer accidental. Our guiding principles and leadership vision help us find people who will resonate and fit in the organizations we are creating. They can also serve as a filter for which clients to accept.

When we communicate our leadership vision, it inspires the behavior we want. Our teams begin to embody the qualities of our personal stories and our organization's culture. Our cultures become a competitive differentiator. We see clear examples of this in Silicon Valley. The quirks of the founders and their life experiences inform their purpose, their culture, and their guiding principles. Their personal experiences may have taught them that failure is an option and that big wins usually happen when they're also willing to take big leaps. These leaders, in turn, create businesses built on cultures that welcome creativity or embrace failure. Those who will join them on their endeavors are birds of a feather. They find their own people and this is the perfect alchemy for great things to happen.

When we are deliberate about our leadership vision, we have an anchor. It becomes harder to drift. Leaders who are not self-aware or taking the time to regularly check themselves against their vision and guiding principles or to reinforce them with their team are at risk of being surprised by low employee engagement scores, feedback that does not align with their self-perception, and/or employees who behave in ways that spoil the culture, the firm's reputation, or ability to attract great people.

A Vision for Your Business

With our guiding principles clarified and communicated and our leadership vision in place, we can be confident that any business plans or people who are added to this foundation will have a much higher chance of success. The advisory firms we see endure have one more unwavering quality: They are clear about their purpose. Graham Kenny, the managing director of Strategic Factors, a Sydney, Australia-based consultancy, defines a purpose as what inspires your staff to do good work. It is how you can express your organization's impact on the lives of whoever you're trying to serve. It's what makes them feel it.[2]

The advisory firms that succeed have found the balance of holding tight to their core, unchanging values, principles, and purpose while simultaneously and optimistically moving forward no matter what challenging circumstances lurk.

In our industry, there is no shortage of opportunity. We can look to capture an entirely new base of clients. We can focus our efforts on improving our business's efficiency and embrace the exciting new technologies that are transforming this industry. We can look to merge with or acquire firms as another means to grow. We can focus on our communities and developing those who will come next.

There is no shortage of opportunity, but from our experience, the businesses that endure are businesses that look at each opportunity through the lens of their values, leadership vision, and the purpose they have set for their business. A purpose is the "why" behind the vision for your business. It's the "why" you pursue some opportunities and it is what makes passing on others easy.

Like our guiding principles and our leadership vision, understanding the purpose behind your business takes time and introspection to develop. When we do it well, we get more than a mission statement or slogan to hang on the wall. We get a framework through which to make important decisions about our business. We have a tool to know what to invest in that will bring us the outcomes we want and what to say no to.

Consider the vision of these widely known organizations:

- Merck's vision, which they have followed since 1950, is to bring the best of medicine to each and every person.
- Sam Walton's was to make quality products available to ordinary people.
- Stanford's was to be the Harvard of the West.

These leaders had a vision for their business and they used that vision to guide their decisions and investments since their business's inception. They used it to achieve their goals, strengthen relationships, and stay relevant to their clients, employees, and communities. Knowing our purpose puts us in a much stronger position to set our priorities and actions, filter out the distractions, and align our resources to help our businesses flourish.

The businesses that succeed know how to keep their guiding principles, leadership vision, and organizational purpose fixed in spite of changing markets. The businesses that succeed know how to stay resolute in their

---

[2] https://hbr.org/2014/09/your-companys-purpose-is-not-its-vision-mission-or-values.

principles and purpose and also know how to endlessly adapt to the changes happening around them.

We now know how important it is to have discipline to understand what in our business is core to who we are and what is fixed in terms of our values, purpose, and principles. But how do we adapt to the changes, challenges, and opportunities that exist for us in the moment? We think it begins with envisioning our future and communicating it in a way that it becomes a shared vision.

A Vision Toolkit

Confused about the terminology? The following is from Graham Kenny's HBS article,* annotated by the authors. We believe each of these exercises is an opportunity to engage your team, sharpen your focus, and more intimately understand why your business does what it does.

A vision statement says what the organization wishes to be like in some years' time. It presents what we do beyond our day-to-day activity in a clear, memorable way.

A mission statement describes what business the organization is in (and what it is not). It balances the present and the future. It provides focus for the leadership team and its employees. It's a tool that can help a firm narrow the type of work it does and the clients it serves. Waldron Private Wealth articulates this simply on their website, noting it is in the business of "Providing custom wealth management strategies to highly compensated executives, professionals, business owners, and inheritors of wealth."

Guiding principles give employees a set of directions that inform how the department or organization operates. Think of tools like customer care principles or Caroline O'Connell's list from earlier in this chapter. It helps employees think about more than *what* we do; it illuminates for them *how*.

Purpose is different in that it's outward focused; it's motivational; it connects the heart and the head of an organization. It provides the intrinsic motivation to your organization. It is what lights up your staff to do good work with no prodding and without an excessive focus on extrinsic motivators like compensation. Kenny notes these examples in his article:
- The financial services company, ING: Empowering people to stay a step ahead in life and in business.
- The Kellogg food company: Nourishing families so they can flourish and thrive.
- The insurance company IAG: To help people manage risk and recover from the hardship of unexpected loss.

---

* https://hbr.org/2014/09/your-companys-purpose-is-not-its-vision-mission-or-values.

Ability to Translate Vision into Action

The second characteristic we noted that the best leaders in the business of financial advice have is knowing how to translate their vision into action. Some leaders attempt to get results by mirroring leaders they had.

Key to translation is having benchmarks by which one measures progress. Critical areas of data to track include client engagement, employee engagement, business development, relationship management, financial and operating performance, and risk management. Once you define the key elements of success in each category, the metrics to measure progress become obvious.

Generationally, the leaders of today's businesses were more prone to experiencing the leadership style of stern parents or military heroes. This style of leadership tended to be heavy-handed, top down, and hierarchical.

While we may get action and results with this style of leadership, we may not win the hearts and minds of the people who are giving their time and energy to help us achieve our goals. Not surprisingly, this kind of leadership is often found in organizations with high attrition, little loyalty, and where misuses of power, grandiosity, and a lack of humility reign.

Another approach to translating our vision into action and getting results is a more conscious style of leadership. Pershing's study *Americans Crave a New Kind of Leader*[3] compared traditional models of leadership with newer styles.

We surveyed the American public, and by a landslide, Americans, across demographics and genders, prefer the kind of leaders who abandon authority and favor service; for the kind of leaders who eschew efficiency and process and favor innovation and self-renewal; and for the kind of leaders who listen more than they talk—and listen differently.

New model leaders are listening to their teams for input on how to develop and execute plans. They are considering their team's input as they make key decisions.

Perhaps what is most different, though, is how these new model leaders are listening more subtly, how they are attending to the well-being of their organization, developing a deep awareness about their team, the environment they are working in, and themselves as leaders. In the past, one was appointed to lead. New model leaders understand that today, we must think and act differently to earn the right to lead.

---

[3] https://www.pershing.com/_global-assets/pdf/americans-crave-a-new-kind-of-leader.pdf.

FIGURE 12.1 Americans want a new kind of leader

Below are several pairs of qualities that a leader may have. In each pair, please choose which quality you think a leader in a Fortune 500 company should have.

	Traditional Leadership Qualities		Newer, More Collaborative Leadership Qualities		
	General Population	Employed	General Population	Employed	
Talk, give orders, and answer questions	22%	22%	78%	78%	Listen, consult, and ask questions
Reward, threat, and demand compliance	20%	19%	80%	81%	Discern others' needs, coach, facilitate, and generate commitment
Create and respect hierarchies	27%	26%	73%	74%	Foster networks and communities
Efficiency through routine/mechanization	19%	21%	81%	79%	Innovation through creativity/lifelong learning and self-renewal
Command and control	38%	42%	62%	58%	Service to others

▨ Significantly Higher
Source:

This kind of self-awareness is a critical first step to translate our vision into action, or said more directly—get others to take positive action on our behalf.

With this information we can move toward establishing and communicating a shared vision. Creating a shared vision requires us to be forward-looking. It requires us to combine our dreams, purpose, mission, and goals together in a way that inspires others.

This may have always been the case, but it is more acute as principled Millennials joined our ranks. Leaders need to make sure that there is something in their vision that creates the promise of a better tomorrow as a result of doing the work.

It is our belief that being able to tap into this intrinsic need we all have, and communicate it with a shared vision, will garner much stronger results than any other mechanism we have to encourage a particular behavior.

Let's explore this for a moment. For traditional leaders, it is not only their style of leadership that feels out of date. It is also the tools and means they use to motivate others. For years, Mark has had the belief, albeit a controversial one in the financial services industry, that compensation is not in itself a motivation factor but rather a means to recognize motivated people who do their jobs well.

Clayton Christensen, a business professor at Harvard who wrote *The Innovator's Dilemma*, identifies compensation as a hygiene factor along with status, job security, and work conditions. In other words, a fair compensation plan is necessary to keep people engaged and on task, but by itself does not drive positive behavior. He identifies motivation factors such as challenging work, recognition, responsibility, and opportunities for personal growth.

Researchers in human motivation validate Christensen's argument. Known as intrinsic and extrinsic motivations, it's the difference between people doing things as a result of their own internal desire and excitement or doing things to achieve a tangible reward or punishment (for example, a sales bonus or no bonus). Daniel Pink and others have studied human motivation and the research seems clear: External (carrot and stick) motivators do produce results; they just might not be the most inspiring results. Carrot and stick motivators generally result in compliance; getting the job done to spec; and sometimes they are the catalyst for negative outcomes, encouraging people to cheat or take unnecessary risks to hit the target or achieve the goal.[4]

Intrinsic motivation is where passion, innovation, and a desire to do good thrive. Work done from a place of self-motivation is always superior work. We support Dan Pink's and Clay Christensen's recommendations: Pay people well. In fact, pay them more than enough so that money is not a distraction. Then, think about how to shift from extrinsic motivational tools (compensation, compliance) to intrinsic ones, like providing opportunities to master complex tasks, learn new things, have autonomy and innovate, get better as a professional and as a person.

For example, if external factors worked consistently, then broker-dealers who pay their registered reps on a compensation grid would have only top revenue producers. If RIA firms use incentive bonuses to encourage their people to get new clients, then these firms would be drowning in opportunity.

The revelation here is that incentive plans reward those who were already motivated to accomplish the goal, not necessarily to cause them to pursue the goal. There are exceptions, of course, but it has become painfully obvious in watching companies that use money as a substitute for management that they ultimately end up creating an expectation that what gets done requires a treat at the end.

Rather, Dan Pink encourages managers to reflect on where they spend their time and effort. Are we spending our time developing elaborate incentive

---

[4] https://hbr.org/2010/02/what-motivates-us

schemes or recognizing and celebrating our team's progress? Can we challenge our leadership team to focus less on the carrot and stick motivators and instead give our teams more autonomy, more ways to express their passions, and more of a sense of purpose?

The leaders we admire most have a passion for something other than making money and status. They want to make a difference in the world. It's difficult to ask others to do what we are not doing ourselves. It is difficult to ask employees to care for clients as they would their own families if we made it clear we value profits over them. If we talk about a work-life balance, but never leave the office, have poor health and relationships ourselves, we simply cannot be credible in our offer of it to others. If we say we value creativity and innovation, but conduct performance reviews around process, standards, and hours billed, we have an integrity conflict: What we say, do, think, and how we act are not in harmony.

When we know our intrinsic purpose—when we know what lights us up and we set out to share it with the world, others can come along, too. Our employees can only have willingness and conviction when we do, and that begins with finding and sharing a common purpose for your business and then creating the environment to really let others participate in creating it.

Ownership and Accountability

The third trait of exceptional leaders are those who manage to get out of the way and create a sense of ownership and accountability within their organizations. Mark is known for saying we cannot motivate people—only demotivate them. In our experience, the fastest way to demotivate your team is to take away their sense of ownership, accountability, and personal responsibility.

When we say we want people to act like owners, there's an inherent paradox presented. Ownership implies someone has it or doesn't. You're an owner or you're not—and if you're not, there's a feeling that the buck stops with someone else. It's not enough to tell people to act like an owner. You cannot anoint them with the responsibility. You have to collaborate with them so they develop this quality themselves.

The first place to start is to look at the level of trust in your organization. It's not enough to provide our teams with the tools they need to do their job—a nice office space, the latest technology, or training. If we do not trust our colleagues and employees to do good work, they simply can't deliver it.

To demonstrate trust, it again begins with how we show up. We need to be leaders who start with the assumption that things will go right, not be on the lookout for what will go wrong. We need to notice and praise the good. We need to be open-minded to new ways of doing things, not insisting on our way of doing things.

We need to be leaders who open our doors, encourage questions, know how to make our teams feel safe, and take calculated risks without fear of repercussions.

We need to be leaders who insist on others collaborating.

Collaboration increases the level of personal accountability people feel within our organizations. We start to have expectations of each other and we begin to not want to let the other down. When we think of each other as competent and deliver on our promises, when our words and actions align, a beautiful thing happens. Trust happens.

One of our favorite quotes is attributed to a now-infamous private school headmaster, Jean Harris: "The greatest indignity that one person can commit against another is to underestimate them. We do this by expecting little of them."

Here are some ways we can build trust and the ownership mentality that follows.

- **Open communications.** Encourage face-to-face interactions, one-on-one weekly meetings, and skip meetings with the reports of your reports. Block your calendar to dedicate time to meet regularly with your team as individuals, groups, and walking the hall to check in, see the faces of your team, and notice the vibe.
- **Demolish hierarchy.** Whether in communications or decision making, insisting on protocol for who can talk to who, or who makes decisions. While the holacracy Zappos introduced (organizations without management or titles) may be too much too soon for some organizations, the idea is compelling. Distribute decision making and give everyone the opportunity to work on what they do best. Play to their strengths. Information is easily accessible; issues are dealt with in the open; cross-functional teams are intentional to cross-train employees and cross-pollinate their thinking and perspectives. In organizations of the past, to talk to someone, receive information, or partner with them, you needed permission, to CC a manager, and maybe, if you were lucky, you had a serendipitous meeting with the founder or leadership team. This did not create trust,

agility, or connections and innovation. It created bottlenecks, politicking, and silos.

- **Let those experiencing the conflict solve it.** Triangulation is when two people experience a conflict, but we let a third person solve it. None of us like to have hard and difficult conversations, but when we avoid them or allow others to take a bypass, it diminishes trust in our organizations. It also robs people of an opportunity to develop this critical skill of professional courage. As leaders, we need to be impeccable with our word. We need to walk our talk. Have direct conversations; don't complain to anyone or speak about the conflict other than with who is involved. When employees come to you to mediate and help solve their problems, help them have the professional courage they need by sending them back to the person they need to work it out with. Train your staff on conflict management, negotiation, and trust building.
- **Ask, don't tell.** Ensuring people feel ownership means valuing their opinion and ideas. Really valuing it. That means instead of providing direction, we ask how they would approach and solve a problem. We let them know that we value their creativity and new thinking, and condemn thinking with reasons based on "But that's the way we have always done it." Rather than providing direction, exceptional leaders are asking questions like: Do you have the training and support you need? What challenges can I remove? What problems can I help you solve?
- **Be transparent and share information.** Too often leaders withhold transparent and open communications. They sit on bad news, fail to address what their teams are speculating on, and allow important news to spread rather than address it head on. Another behavior we see tolerated is withholding information or resources. For example, when working with a large financial services firm, the technology team wanted direct access to clients to hear their feedback and insights. The client-facing team withheld this access, afraid of how the technology team would present the situation, and afraid that they would not look knowledgeable and thereby negatively affect the relationship. Management tolerated this and ultimately, the negative impact to the relationship arose, not because the technology team somehow embarrassed the client-facing team, but because the solutions failed to keep up as a result of this blocked access.
- **Know that a feedback engine is a growth engine.** We cannot truly know the impact of our work unless we see it through the impact we make on the people around us. We need feedback as leaders and we need to develop a culture of it in our organizations. Feedback should be normalized, a part of our everyday interactions, not something shared once or twice a year in

performance appraisals. Help others learn tools for delivering it and managing their feelings receiving it. Teach others to reframe feedback from feeling criticized to someone caring enough to invest in their success and their future potential.

- **Increase responsibility to increase accountability.** Clients surveyed in our satisfaction surveys frequently note the desire for more first call resolution. Nothing is more frustrating than being put on hold or waiting through a lengthy resolution period to get a manager's approval to solve a simple problem. We encourage everyone in the firm from compliance officers and desktop support to actual client-facing individuals to see their role as serving the client. If one function dawdles or is unresponsive, the whole service model unravels. Everyone needs to see their role in serving the client and everyone needs to be empowered to do what's right without exceptions and supervisor approvals. It all comes back to trust, so where you can trust, be sure to do so: Increase the authority your employees have to resolve client concerns or complaints, reduce approvals, use technology to reduce routine and boring work, eliminate busywork like status reports and scorecards where you can, allow others to use their judgment, and reward creative problem solving. Broaden job descriptions or eliminate them to avoid the "It's not my job" syndrome.
- **Acknowledge and recognize.** We referred to Caroline O'Connell's guiding principles earlier. Point Seven is "Strive for excellence in all that you do." Behind this principle is Caroline's deep belief in and expectation of her team to deliver their best. Caroline has high expectations for herself and her team. She frequently hires opportunistically, before a particular need arises, with an eye toward raising the bar and disrupting the status quo. Caroline has managed to make her team feel comfortable with this, knowing new joiners were not coming to displace anyone but to strengthen the team overall. Caroline knows how to bring out the best in people by *seeing them.* Not unlike Michelangelo, who is credited with saying all he was doing was "freeing the statue from the stone." Caroline takes a similar approach. She has a knack for seeing someone's gifts and freeing them from the stone around them: a lack of self-confidence, fear, or anything else that doesn't serve them. Caroline is quick to recognize the efforts of these individuals who deliver. Caroline gets close to her team. She knows the names of the spouses and children of her employees. She knows what motivates each individual and connects individually with them in the ways that are most meaningful to them. Caroline balances personal and public recognition and knows it need not be pomp and circumstance—she knows the power of a sincere "Thank you" and smile and delivers both often.

Empathy

The fourth trait we suggest exemplary leaders have is empathy. Advisory firm owners and leaders are competent in their craft. They know how to orchestrate financial plans for families, manage their money, and develop relationships. However, in our view, too many leaders stop short here when reflecting on their overall effectiveness.

Our culture provides many examples of leaders who are insensitive about their impact on others. Too often we dismiss crass behavior as an excuse for brilliance. There are well-known examples coming out of Silicon Valley that have founders who fit this bill and who have achieved tremendous financial success and fame (no matter who was left in their wake).

We argue that today's best leaders are not willing to view their success so one-dimensionally. We believe that today's best leaders measure their success by the quality of their relationships and their impact on the people around them above all else.

How do we get good at relationships? It begins with the relationship we have with ourselves. Deepak Chopra notes that great leaders are "beneath no one and above no one." Pause here and think about how you relate to members of your team or people you connect with in our industry, clients, their children, and your life. Are you immune to status and externals? Are you present and warm to everyone you come in contact with? Do you reward behaviors that build relationships across and deep in the organization, not just up?

Building our empathy muscle begins with being present. It's about making the person in front of you feel like he or she has your full attention and that he or she is the most important person in the world. Too often, we signal that even though we've paused what we're doing to talk, we'd really rather be elsewhere. We are looking at our phones or glancing at messages as they come in. We scan the room for who is there instead of making eye contact and dive into the conversation we're having. How about our body language and voice? Are we warm and inviting? Are we even-keeled or do we let our stress, worry, and anger show? Having equanimity means being just as balanced when we express happy moments. Is our joy in check or do we take people on our highs and lows?

To build strong relationships, we need to be genuinely interested in how our employees or clients or colleagues feel. We need to be willing to understand how *they* see things. Withholding this kind of curiosity about the lives and feelings of others creates a pause, leaving them to wonder if we really care about them as people or if we just care about using their talents and time as a means to achieve *our* goals.

Many of us struggle to show empathy. Many of us did not have models of warm adults and authority figures. We also struggle because it takes effort and self-awareness. When we commit to empathy and great relationships, we can no longer show up as unabashed versions of ourselves. Feedback sessions and tools can help, but mostly developing our empathy sensitivity comes when we start to measure our lives not by the KPIs we achieve, but by the hearts we touch.

Developing our empathy skills is not only important for our interactions, but for our clients, too. We often think about our clients in terms of how we experience them. How often do we turn the tables and think about their experiences with us, our staff, our process, and our results?

We could look at nearly every function and put an empathy lens over it. How does it feel to fill out a stack of forms? Be surprised by a tax bill? Receive multiple e-mails each week? Have a relationship manager who doesn't connect and communicate in the ways they would appreciate or really tune in to their needs?

Here are some quick tips to build empathy:

- **Listen:** Sometimes the best thing we can do if we want to build a relationship is do nothing. Too many of us listen to do something. We listen for content. We listen for something we can fix so that we can move on to the next thing. Marshall Rosenberg, psychologist and founder of Nonviolent Communication[5], defines listening as "Our ability to be present to what's really going on within—to the unique feelings and needs a person is experiencing in that very moment."

- **Be vulnerable.** Disclosure is required from both parties for a relationship to really be a trusting and lasting one. Those of us in leadership roles become more relatable and more human to our teams when our challenges and struggles are visible, when they know we didn't just arrive in the positions we have. Sharing these kinds of moments and the feelings (self-doubt, fear, worry) that often accompanied them can connect us to people and help others be stronger on their path. It is helpful to know one is not alone in their challenges or feelings. Too often we see being vulnerable as being weak. This is a misnomer. The opposite is what's true, but as a result, we tend to play it safe in our relationships. We build walls; we are addicted to our busyness; we hide behind formality, texts, or e-mails, all to avoid the risk of opening up. It's not weak to drop these masks. Nothing could take more strength or courage than responding to another in openhearted ways,

---

[5] http://greatergood.berkeley.edu/article/item/six_habits_of_highly_empathic_people1.

and nothing can create a stronger bond or sense of appreciation among colleagues and clients than when people commit to being real.

• **Think of your clients as people.** Too often we hear expressions like my niche, my target market, business-to-business. Analysis will always have its place when running a business. But when we really think about the best ways to serve our clients and build a compelling business model, we must look beyond market segmentation models and client behaviors. We must look at them as people who are trying to meet core needs. The need to feel safe, to trust, to feel their financial well-being is intact. To work together in a way that's not cumbersome or too time consuming, in a way that lets them enjoy their lives and the interactions with us as their financial professional. Remembering that clients, employees, and colleagues are people trying to meet their needs and desires for financial well-being, connection, and safety is one of the best ways to relate and build empathy.

Deepak Chopra brings Eastern wisdom to business in his book *The Soul of Leadership.* Here are three tips from his book that are worth emulating to stay close to your team and to resonate as a leader.

1. Be completely present in the moment. Make those you interact with feel that they are the most important person in that moment.
2. Be responsive to feedback but immune to both criticism and flattery. Do not be offended by criticism and do not let your actions be influenced by flattery.
3. Radiate warmth through compassion, empathy, joy, and equanimity.

Have a core belief that their very best employee is more important than their very best client.

A core belief that their very best employee is more important than their very best client

The last leadership quality that we will explore is the belief that our very best employee is more important than our very best client. It may be counterintuitive to value employees over clients. After all, our clients are the ones who pay our bills and who fund our growth. Furthermore, most advisory firms operate under the mantra of "client first," the implication being that you all will do whatever is necessary to fulfill a client's expectations, even if it is somewhat unreasonable.

But not every decision in this business can be put through a financial filter alone. To appreciate the value of employees over clients, we need to recognize that without them we would not have the capacity to grow, nor the ability to deliver a great client experience, or in some cases, the technical qualifications to do some of the things we do.

Furthermore, every employee represents a point of leverage. The single biggest inhibitor to growth in the advisory business is the lack of capacity to take in more business. Technology helps, of course, but in the end, this is a people business. Even the great technology companies like Google, Apple, Microsoft, and IBM don't operate with robots alone. Rather, they employ thousands of folks to help them innovate and execute on their plans.

To put an even finer point on this argument, most advisors we know have a go-to person in their business. There is usually someone to whom they turn for an opinion, or to get things done. There is often someone who knows the details of the business and where to look for important pieces of information. These individuals often have the pulse of the rest of the staff and are able to guide the leader in how they relate to employees.

But often, though, these are the people many leaders take most for granted. Like your dominant hand, it's there when you need to pick up something, or open the door, or turn the screw cap on your bottle of beer. Imagine how difficult these quotidian functions would be without the use of that hand.

It's easy to give lip service to the value these key people bring to your firm. You'll thank them publicly at different events; you'll wish them happy birthday or send them to conferences, but how do you interact with them throughout the day?

Imagine that you are in the middle of a highly anguished, tear-filled conversation with this employee over his high level of frustration over something. In the middle of this rant, your biggest, richest client calls to speak with you. What do you do?

Imagine that your largest client is also verbally abusive to your staff. One day, he comes into your office and lets loose on your best employee with a stream of vulgarities and insults. What do you do?

Imagine that this key employee has been planning to take his kids to see their favorite performer and the date has been in the calendar for months. When the day arrives, you tell him he must stay to get something done because one of your top clients needs a report in the morning. What do you do?

We could identify a thousand hypothetical examples but you have probably lived many of them already. The question is whether you are showing your hand every day as to who is most important to your business.

Those leaders who recognize the value of their most important employee over their most important client derive great benefit from the loyalty they engender, and the respect they show.

Index

Printed and bound by CPI Group (UK) Ltd, Croydon, CR0 4YY

16/04/2025

14658449-0001

.